WOMEN CLERGY IN ENGLAND

Sexism, Modern Consciousness, and Church Viability

WOMEN CLERGY IN ENGLAND

Sexism, Modern Consciousness, and Church Viability

Edward C. Lehman, Jr.

Studies in Religion and Society
Volume 16

The Edwin Mellen Press
Lewiston/Queenston

BV
676
.L433 **Library of Congress Cataloging-in-Publication Data**
1987
Lehman, Edward C.
Women clergy in England.

(Studies in religion and society ; v. 16)
Bibliography: p.
Includes index.
1. Women clergy--England--Public opinion. 2. Public opinion--
England. I. Title. II. Series.
BV676.L427 1987 305.4'32 86-28547
ISBN 0-88946-858-3

This is volume 16 in the continuing series
Studies in Religion and Society
Volume 16 ISBN 0-88946-858-3
SRS Series ISBN 0-88946-863-X

The Edwin Mellen Press   The Edwin Mellen Press
Box 450   Box 67
Lewiston, New York   Queenston, Ontario
USA 14092   L0S 1L0 CANADA

Printed in the United States of America

to Johnnie
skillful teacher
wise confidante
loving companion

TABLE OF CONTENTS

LIST OF TABLES AND FIGURES

PREFACE

This book is the result of an empirical study of a social movement especially visible today in the United States and the United Kingdom -- the effort to modify traditional sex roles in institutionalized religion. For centuries in Western societies the everyday assumption has been that men and not women are the priests, ministers, and rabbis. Since the 1960's many women (joined by a few men) have questioned this arrangement by demanding their legitimate place in the ranks of ordained clergy. Some have succeeded. Others have failed.

While the theological and philosophical battles associated with these events have gone on for nearly a quarter century now, it is only recently that anyone bothered to ask what the lay church members thought about the issue. The denominational hierarchy apparently assumed that, since they were the experts in such matters, it really wasn't important to consult with the people in the pews. No one seemed to care what they thought. However, the last several years have witnessed efforts to correct that situation, and this book is one of them. It reports on a study of lay church members' responses to the women-in-ministry movement.

This report is unique in yet another way, for it deals with the situation in the United Kingdom. To date nearly all of the empirical studies of women in ministry have been done in the United States. This undertaking extended that work to England and made possible some direct comparisons which were not available previously. Now for the first time we have a picture of what ordinary church members all over England think about the advent of ordained women clergy.

Although one person's name is typically associated with a book like this (someone has to take responsibility

xv

for it), it is common knowledge that most authors depend heavily on the support of many other people. Without that underpinning, few good books would appear. This volume is no exception. The scope of this study was so broad that it called for the support of more organizations and individuals than usual. I must acknowledge my indebtedness to all of them.

The research in England was made possible, first of all, by the generosity of the State University of New York, College at Brockport, and the Sociology Department there. They supported the work by approving my sabbatical leave for the academic year 1983-84, making it possible for me to spend the year in the United Kingdom to do the national survey. They subsequently also provided computer services for analyzing the data, and they gave me the services of a highly competent secretary in the person of Ms. Gloria Condoluci, whose skill is exceeded only by her forbearance.

It was also necessary to have a useful base of operations for the research once in England. The solution to that problem came from the Department of Sociology at the University of Exeter, who bestowed on me the position of Honorary Research Fellow for the year. The individual most directly involved in that arrangement was Dr. Barry Turner, Head of the Sociology Department and Dean of the Faculty at Exeter. Thanks, Barry!

Another individual at Exeter whose support was indispensable to the success of the research is Dr. Margaret Hewitt, a sociologist who is also deeply involved personally in the General Synod of the Church of England. While Dr. Hewitt and I disagree profoundly about the merits of women's ordination itself, she separated that personal stance from her professional position as a colleague and offered her assistance most generously. The result was a set of procedural keys that opened more doors in the Church of England than I would have known to do alone. I am deeply indebted to you, Margaret.

I must also acknowledge the critical assistance of two seasoned survey researchers in England whose advice contributed decisively to the success I had in sampling and data collection. These persons are Dr. Robert Towler of the Independent Broadcast Authority and Mr. John Hanvey of the Harris polling organization. They pulled me away from my American assumptions about doing survey research and oriented me to the realities of the British scene. It might have been disaster without their counsel. Thanks, guys!

Survey research costs money, sometimes a lot of it. And even though I pulled this one off on a shoestring, I still needed assistance in this area. Several organizations provided financial support for this undertaking. I am indebted to the Society for the Scientific Study of Religion for the research grant they gave me to help cover research expenses. I also owe a debt of gratitude to administrators of three of the denominations involved in the project, all three of whom contributed enough money to support the data-collection efforts among their own members. These persons include Dr. Geoffrey Russling of the Department of Ministry in the Baptist Union of Britain and Ireland; Mr. Trevor T. Rowe, Division of Ministries of the Methodist Church; and Ms. Margaret Taylor of the Education Department of the United Reformed Church. I hope they are satisfied that their trust was justified. Finally, I am grateful to Ms. Ann DuBois of the Vocation Agency of the United Presbyterian Church (USA) for a research grant covering travel and other expenses in England. Heartfelt thanks to you all!

Scholars worth their salt will also admit that their dependence on others goes far beyond finances. There are countless conversations and letters in the context of which one's ideas are explored and sharpened. I was fortunate to have many such experiences. For fear of omitting someone who helped me in this way, I hesitate to list those who come to mind, but I must identify many such individuals who helped immensely merely by listening, reading, commenting on rough drafts, and discussing the issues with me. First among these are several persons "in the trenches" of the women-in-ministry encounters. These include two key individuals in the Movement for the Ordination of Women -- Ms. Margaret Webster and Deaconess Diana McClatchey. I received similar assistance from The Reverend Ms. Connie Lockwood of South Street Baptist Church in Exeter and from Ms. Mary Tanner of the Board of Mission and Unity of the Church of England. Colleagues who rendered similar services include Professors Nancy Nason-Clark, Barbara Hargrove, Larry Petersen, Jackson W. Carroll, Beth E. Vanfossen, Fred Halley, Benton Johnson, and Alan Black.

In the final analysis, of course, it is my own work and judgement that is reflected in the pages which follow, and I must take responsibility for it. I do so with the confidence that I have presented the best picture of English church members' receptivity to clergywomen available. Yet I also know that even more accurate portrayals will be soon to follow. And that's good.

Edward C. Lehman, Jr.
Brockport, New York
December, 1986

WOMEN CLERGY IN ENGLAND

Sexism, Modern Consciousness, and Church Viability

CHAPTER 1
NEW SHEPHERDS

According to herding folklore, in some parts of the world where shepherds still personally tend their sheep as of old, there is an unusual bond between the sheep and the person who cares for them. The animals recognize the voice of their shepherd. The shepherds sing to pass the time as they lead their flocks to and from pasture and while they watch as the sheep graze and rest. The sheep learn to distinguish their shepherd's voice from the sounds of strangers.

This imprinting is said to pacify the animals. Hearing the familiar voice while grazing, the sheep seem to be content as though they recognize the presence of a protector. The voice also gives direction. When in transit the sheep learn to follow the herder by simply moving in the direction of that sound.

This tidy order becomes unglued, however, when sheep change hands as they must do quite often. Animals are sold, bartered, or passed to others as gifts or inheritances. By whatever device of exchange, some animals find themselves in the presence of a new and unfamiliar shepherd. They do not hear the voice that once signified security and gave direction. They must adjust to new sounds. Confused and unsettled, they must be coaxed and prodded to accept the sounds of a new shepherd. It can be a difficult transition.

A CHANGE IN THE MINISTRY

This book is about another kind of shepherd and flock. It deals with clergy and the congregations they serve -- ministers and their charges. It is concerned with a change they are experiencing, the introduction of a new kind of shepherd. Many congregations are learning that their pastor's voice won't always sound as it has in the past. The traditional baritone range characteristic of the clergy is being supplemented by an unfamiliar treble sound -- the voice of a woman.

Women are entering the ranks of ordained clergy. This movement can be seen in most "mainline" Protestant denominations and in Reform and Conservative Judaism. Even in some religious bodies where women's ordination has not been approved as yet, women are pressing their respective hierarchies for change and acceptance as regular ordained priests and ministers. These pressures are apparent in the Roman Catholic Church, the Church of England, and in many evangelical and otherwise conservative religious communities. This entry of women into clergy ranks represents a major change in religious leadership in the Judaeo-Christian tradition.

A Study of Lay Reactions

This work examines some of the ways in which lay church members are responding to these developments. Their reactions can be as different as night and day. Some members adjust quickly -- like those sheep who take but little time to learn to follow the new shepherd's voice. Indeed some laypersons cry, "It's about time!" They see such reforms as long overdue. Other members, however, have greater difficulty getting accustomed to the concept of female pastoral leadership. Not unlike some other flocks, they apparently need to be coaxed and prodded a great deal to recognize the new voice of the clergy.

In the chapters which follow, we shall examine the results of a study of reactions to women in ministry on the part of lay members of four Protestant denominations in England -- the Church of England, the Baptist Union, the Methodist Church, and the United Reformed Church. These groups make up the majority of Protestant church members in that country, and their responses to the women-in-ministry issue reflect the effects of several characteristics of their society. A comparison of the British data with parallel observations in the United States reinforces this point. Yet we shall also see denominational differences in the members' reactions to the clergywoman issue, variations which reflect important divergences in their social location and cultural traditions. Many of these patterns resemble what one would expect to see intuitively. But there are also some surprises -- varying modes of response to women in ministry that suggest some new insights into the social and cultural identities of the church members involved.

CHANGES IN CULTURAL CONTEXT

The movement of women into the ordained ministry is a predictable reflection of much broader changes occurring in British life which "came to a head" and expressed themselves in this particular form in roughly the last quarter century. These alterations in society have been variously labelled the effects of urbanization, industrialization, modernization, and secularization. By whatever label, processes such as these have resulted in what Berger calls a transformation of consciousness (Berger, et al, 1973). As a result of the rationalization of economic and political life, coupled with proliferations of culture contacts either directly or through mass media, people's awareness of their own identity, their institutions, and the global scene has been relativized. As a result today many ideologies, values, and roles are taken for granted less and less. Instead of viewing social life as given, some people increasingly see it as arbitrary and malleable. The challenge to the male "death grip" on the ministry springs in part from this perspective on social life. It is a manifestation of "modern consciousness."

The most thorough treatments of "modernity" and its individual, institutional, and societal dimensions have been by Peter Berger and his collaborators (see, for example, Berger, 1969; Berger, et al, 1973; and Berger, 1977). In these discussions, modern consciousness is treated as <u>secularized consciousness</u>. The modern era has also been a secularized period. By the term "secular," I do not mean "irreligous," "apostate," "worldly," or other synonyms which have been criticized appropriately as involving unacceptable assumptions about the nature of societies past, present, or future (see, for example, Shiner, 1967; and Martin, 1978). Instead, I am using the term in the sense which carries the least normative connotations. As a facet of modern consciousness, secularization refers to a process of taking a skeptical or relativistic posture toward aspects of society and culture previously considered "given" and immalleable. Instead of viewing human institutions as sacred or beyond question, modern secular consciousness relates to them as mundane and open to question. The process of change from the former orientation to the latter one is what we mean by "secularization."

It is fair to say that much secularization begins with industrialization and its rationalization of work. In the name of efficiency and control, traditional ways of thinking and acting in the work place give way to various innovations which maximize profits and minimize losses. New and better ways of producing and distributing products become the dominant values of the firm. Companies develop experimentation to promote those values -- a "tinkering" orientation, as Berger puts it (1973: 30). The intrinsic value of tradition is supplanted by the extrinsic value of tinkering with the present in order to increase the likelihood of a predictable and profitable future.

It is also clear that it has been hard to keep those animals in the barn. Once this cognitive style of tinkering with economic institutions is fully grown, it bursts through the doors of economic life and spills over into the rest of the barnyard of society. The secular posture of tinkering, based on relativistic and pragmatic assumptions about institutional values and structures, invades the provinces of traditional patterns in other institutions -- the family, politics, education, leisure, and so forth. Social movements in many areas of life illustrate this broad process. Year by year, fewer and fewer areas of life are taken as given and unquestionable -- capitalist economics, labor unions, two-parent families, public schools, mass communications, modes of transportation, and on and on -- all have experienced the questioning onslaught of the modern cognitive style. "Are these ways of doing things really necessary?"

Changing Sex Roles

The study which we report here deals with but one of those movements. It focuses on the increasing tendency of people to reject the inevitability and immutability of distinctions between the sexes characteristic of western social life in the past -- manifest especially in the women's movement. Sex roles taken for granted by previous generations are breaking down. This shift is also a manifestation of modern consciousness. The secular mind set, as it relativizes modes of production and social organization, also desacralizes very personal things such as individuals' sense of identity. It places high value on concepts of individual worth, autonomy, freedom, and rights. Especially in the late twentieth century, the secular cognitive style has begun to tear the veil separating maleness and femaleness. Men and women are encouraged to scrutinize sexual identity and the traditional role expectations associated with gender and to choose what facets of those identities and roles they want for themselves. As one may choose whether or not be to "efficient," one may also elect how "tough" or "compassionate" one wants to be -- how "masculine" or "feminine."

Signs of these changing patterns of gender are omnipresent. The presence of both sexes in some occupations, for example, has become so commonplace that we hardly notice the distinction any more. Today few people look twice at the sight of a woman police officer (unless they are culpable at the moment, and then it makes no difference that she is a woman). We are also at home with women anchoring national news broadcasts, a recent innovation which at the time brought predictions of disaster which never materialized, of course. We are equally comfortable with the legal counsel of an attorney or solicitor who happens to be a woman, with the prescription for medicine obtained from a woman physician, or the medicine itself prepared by a female pharmacist. In short, few occupations have been untouched by recent secularizing challenges to traditional sex roles, and we seem none the worse for it as a society.

Change in Religious Institutions

Institutionalized religion is an area of life which many observers regard as most hesitant to accept change. Since religious systems constitute the very epitome of the sacred, it is argued, religious systems will be the most reticent to give in to secularizing trends. The routines of church life are anchored in systems of thought which stem from what is considered eternal and "given" -- the very antithesis of modern consciousness. The structures of church organization, the content of religious education, words spoken and music played or sung in congregational worship, and religious codes for daily conduct are all considered slow to change because of their presumed linkage to Divine revelation.

However, it would be very easy to exaggerate this point in view of some recent developments in church life especially in the United States. There is a peculiar quality to the ways in which some religious bodies have changed their corporate life recently. The alacrity with which they have mounted the bandwagons of televangelism, computerized proselytization, mass fund raising, staging theatrical productions, national political campaigns, amending the Constitution in the United States, medical ethics and international relations -- to name just a few -- paints a picture of religious organizations which are anything but reticent to modify their priorities and practices. One must admit in all fairness that these shifts in the life of religious organizations did not involve their basic theology, polity, concept of ministry and similar core areas of their religious traditions. The new ventures could be described as peripheral to their central religious beliefs and rituals, and this caveat is probably appropriate. However, the programmatic

developments do clearly signify shifts in basic agendas --
if not in basic values -- and they serve to render some of
these organizations hardly recognizable to their spiritual
forebears. The past ethos of self-criticism and longing
for moral perfection is hard to find these days, as are
the ascetic actions that often flow from such
orientations. In their place we find an
instrumentalization of religion with its emphasis on
public relations, image management, social reform
movements, and status politics.

In any case, if we assume that at least some aspects
of church life are slow to change, it seems reasonable to
include sex roles in religious systems in that
conservative category. In historical fact, in most
societies participating in the Judaeo-Christian tradition,
religious leadership has been the province of men both
officially and de facto. In some of these communities,
even the involvement of women in the act of corporate
worship itself is severely restricted. Women at times
must occupy separate physical space from the men, refrain
from entering other spaces at any time, keep their hands
off certain religious objects, be generally silent, and be
submissive to the official leadership of the men. Others
are more open to female participation in that they allow
mixed worship, freedom of movement, access to all
religious objects, freedom of expression, and even
positions of responsibility. But even here the official
leaders have been males. To be female in the churches has
also meant being a subservient follower. This fact has
been slow to change.

By the mid 1970's, fundamental changes in sex roles
had taken place in so many sectors of life beyond the
churches that many women within those ecclesiastical
bodies became dissatisfied with traditional sex roles

which seemed to be endemic to religious life. They began to challenge them as morally and theologically indefensible. As of this writing (1986), the actions of these women have gained sufficient support to produce heated discussion of religious sexism, a debate which has manifested itself in the commercial press, in newsprint, in the broadcast media, and in the agendas of denominational deliberative bodies (see, for example, Howard, 1984). The movement has visibility and momentum. It has resulted in the ordination of women in several Protestant religious bodies. It continues to develop organizational pressures for such innovations in other denominations.

SECULAR CONTEXT OF RELIGIOUS CHANGE

Most discussions pro and con of the issue of women's ordination emphasize the Biblical, theological, and historical dimensions of the controversy. This is appropriate, for the changes in question involve positions of leadership within specific religious organizations in the Judaeo-Christian tradition. No doubt the motives and rationale for promoting the ordination of women to the priesthood are based on deep religious commitments and desires to serve the churches in fuller ways than has been possible in the past. It is equally likely that persons opposing women's ordination also view their actions primarily in such a theological frame of reference.

Nevertheless, the available evidence clearly supports the idea that <u>these changes in religious life are to be understood in relation to broader changes taking place in the social context around the churches.</u> As shown below, each period of questioning traditional roles for women in the churches corresponded with a time of more general challenges to accepted sex roles in the larger society. In most of the denominations in the study, the initial impulse for changing women's roles in ministry coincided either with the suffrage movement early in the twentieth century, pragmatic social changes associated with World War II, or especially the women's liberation movement of the 1960's and 70's. In some instances the linkages between the secular and religious movements were explicit, while in other cases the concomitance was the only directly observable fact. However, the evidence is so consistent that it is highly unlikely that the associations between the two arenas of pressures for social change -- the secular and the religious -- are merely coincidental and therefore spurious. The modern secularizing modifications to sex roles in the larger society are most likely causally related to the movements for allowing women to become ordained clergy.

Some of the concomitant variation between secular and religious sex-role change can be seen in the typical timing of developments for women in ministry in the specific denominations examined in this study. Those sequences of events are portrayed in Figure 1 below. In each case, significant events in the movement toward women's ordination were associated with manifestations of changes in women's roles outside of the churches.

The Baptist Union

British Baptists first opened their pulpits to women at the time of women's suffrage, and they made what could be called final adjustments to these redefinitions of women's roles at the time of the more recent women's movement. The first woman minister was appointed in 1918. In 1925 the Baptist Union Council declared that Baptists saw no objection to women ministers, and they decided to include women in the denominational Handbook in a separate list of "Women Pastors." In the following year, "Accredited Deaconesses" (an order begun in 1890) were also listed in the Handbook. Then in 1966, in the atmosphere of the developing secular women's movement, the Council approved rules for enabling Deaconesses to become ministers. The year 1967 saw the results of a large study of "Women in the Service of the Denomination," a report which legitimized once again the status of women as ordained clergy. By the mid-1970's, all active Deaconesses had officially become "ministers," and all women ministers were listed without differentiation in the main "Accredited List" of ministers in the Handbook (Jarman, 1979).

As of 1983 there were 58 Baptist women ministers in Britain, which was about 3% of all ministers in the denomination. Thirty-nine of these ministers were in pastoral charge. Eleven of the 58 were retired. Many of these women had been Deaconesses who had assumed pastoral responsibilities during the Second World War when they experienced a call and tasted the full range of clergy work. In the presence of the social pressures of the secular women's movement, they were able to regularize their status and gain full acceptance as ministers at the denominational level.

The United Reformed Church

The United Reformed Church came into being through organic union of the former Congregational and Presbyterian Churches. Data from the actions of the Congregational Union indicate a sequence of events which also reflects the impact of feminist activities going on

Figure 1. HISTORICAL DEVELOPMENT OF THE WOMEN IN MINISTRY MOVEMENT

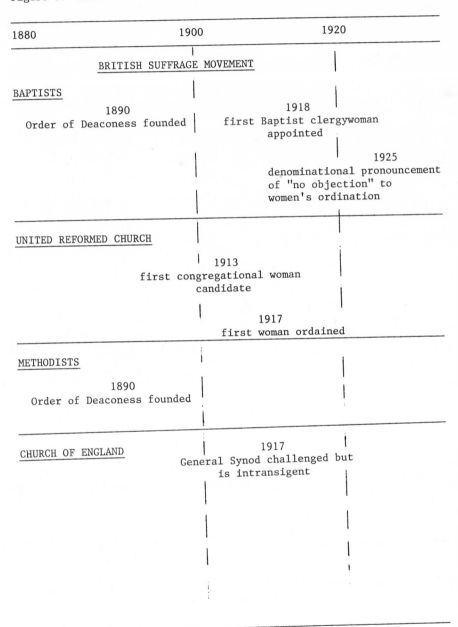

Figure 1. (cont'd.)

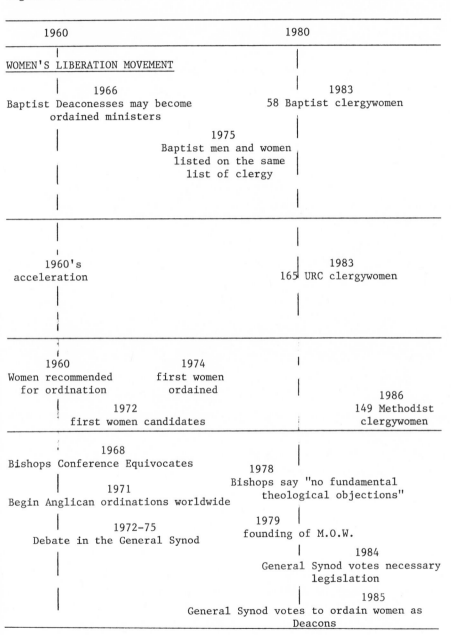

1960		1980

WOMEN'S LIBERATION MOVEMENT

1966
Baptist Deaconesses may become
    ordained ministers

1983
58 Baptist clergywomen

1975
Baptist men and women
listed on the same
list of clergy

1960's
acceleration

1983
165 URC clergywomen

1960   1974
Women recommended   first women
    for ordination   ordained

1972
first women candidates

1986
149 Methodist
clergywomen

1968
Bishops Conference Equivocates

1978
Bishops say "no fundamental
    theological objections"

1971
Begin Anglican ordinations worldwide

1979
founding of M.O.W.

1972-75
Debate in the General Synod

1984
General Synod votes necessary
    legislation

1985
General Synod votes to ordain women as
Deacons

in the surrounding society. In 1900 there were no clergywomen listed in the Congregational Yearbook. A report by Charles A. Haig (1964), a former national leader of the denomination, suggests that the wheels of change for women in the church started rolling in about 1913. At that time the first woman to become a candidate for the ministry gained acceptance as a student at Mansfield College, Oxford. That person was Maude Warden. She completed the course and was ordained in 1917. Up to 1964 she had been followed by 74 other women who had also been ordained. In 1965 there were 61 women on the denominational role of ministers, of whom 34 were in full pastoral charge.

The Haig report (1964) also contains figures from a survey of 54 women clergy in the Congregational Union. Patterns in their responses showed that less than half of the women had experienced obstacles in being accepted for training. Some of them did find that congregations were slow to accept them as pastors. Several Moderators (regional church officials) also said that a number of churches still harbored prejudice against clergywomen. When asked most churches reported that they really still preferred a man in the pulpit. But all agreed that contact with the woman in the role of minister tended to overcome these negative attitudes and that the prevalence of prejudice appeared to be declining. As of 1983, there were 165 women ministers in the United Reformed Church. Most of them were described as being in small and struggling churches. There also still seemed to be a double standard of performance for the clergy -- the woman minister has to perform at a higher level than the male clergy to gain acceptance by the churches.

The Methodist Church

It appears that the doors also started opening for Methodist women wishing to serve as clergy after the feminist movement had made itself felt in other sectors of society. In this instance the major progress awaited the developments of the middle of the twentieth century.

Like the Baptists, the Methodist order of Deaconess started in 1890. But it wasn't until the early 1960's that 38 of these Deaconesses had permission to administer the Sacrament, and even then the arrangement was regarded as a "dispensation" to them. In 1959 the Methodists set up a committee to study the women in ministry issue. The early '60's witnessed formal recommendations for the ordination of women in that body.

The British Methodists actually started ordaining women ministers about ten years later. The first female candidates for ordained ministry were recruited in 1972-73, and the first ordination ceremonies took place at the Bristol conference in 1974. By 1986 the number of women ministers stood at 149, and in that year there were 16 women candidates out of a total of 97 in various stages of training (Rowe, 1986).

The Church of England

In 1986 the Church of England was still struggling with the issue of the ordination of women to the priesthood. They stood alone among the four denominations participating in the study in not recognizing the legitimacy of women's call to the ordained ministry. No doubt a part of this resistance stemmed from their historical association with the Roman Catholic Church and the desire of some members to reestablish that union. The

Catholic Church was also adamantly refusing to take women's ordination seriously. Such traditions have a long history, and many church leaders did not want to discard them hastily.

There is some evidence that the issue of women in ministry arose within the Church of England during the early twentieth century. During the suffrage movement, a Ms. Maude Royden, the eventual founder of the Society for the Ministry of Women in the Church (SMWC), campaigned to improve the role of women in the Anglican Church. In 1917 she became disillusioned with the Church, and she joined the Congregational Union and became a pastor of a church in London. We'll discuss Royden in more detail below, but the point here is simply to note that she and others confronted the Church of England during the suffrage period concerning the ministry of women in that body.

At that point in time, women wishing to study religion seriously had to attend segregated training colleges and had many of the familiar restrictions of dress codes, curfews, etc. Once on the job as church workers, they had stipends and pensions which were far inferior to those of the men. They were generally excluded from any serious leadership roles in the parishes.

These patterns ameliorated somewhat during World War II. As with the other denominations, most able-bodied men were away in the military, and women "lay workers" took over many parish responsibilities. The Canons defining the order of "Deaconess" were enacted in 1941. These deaconesses also took on many clergy chores during the war. In these circumstances, some church women became "Chaplain's Assistants" and served military personnel with the male chaplains. Some of those women report having been accepted as "colleagues" by the chaplains.

Accordingly, many Anglican women had high hopes in 1945-46, but no change was actually forthcoming (SMWC, 1985).

The first woman to be ordained an Anglican priest -- only to have the act nullified later on -- was the Reverend Florence Li Tim Oi. This event took place in China on January 25, 1944. Again under the pressures of wartime conditions, Bishop R. O. Hall of Hong Kong saw a need for competent priestly leadership there, and after months of soul searching ordained the then Deaconess Li Tim Oi an Anglican priest. The regional hierarchy threatened to sanction the bishop over his action, so with the consent of the new priest, the ordination was ignored. Li Tim Oi continued to serve the church, not in the role of deaconess but as a deacon. She did not abjure her Orders but simply ceased to be recognized or to minister as a priest. Her service and symbolic status were recognized in ceremonies in Westminster Abbey on the fortieth anniversary of her ordination.

In 1971, after the more recent women's movement had begun to exert world-wide influence, the issue of women's ordination came up again in the area. This time the Bishop of Hong Kong ordained two women priests, and there was no pressure to rescind the action, so the ordinations remained in effect. The 1948 and 1958 Lambeth Conferences of Anglican bishops had rejected the concept of women's ordination. But by the 1968 conference, the bishops were opening up to the idea and equivocated on it in their statement. They neither approved nor condemned the concept. This equivocation became a green light to the churches in the Anglican communion, and during the 1970's ordinations of women priests took place in several locations.

The Church of England experienced the more forceful pressure to loosen their grip on the ministry with the advent of the women's movement in the 1960's and 70's. Parliament passed the "Sex Discrimination Act" during that period. The law prohibited any sex discrimination by any agency of the British government, thus taking a stance very similar to positions assumed in other parts of the world. However, the Church of England had Parliament draft a special exemption clause which was incorporated into the Act to avoid the application of the law to the Anglican priesthood. Parliament thus exempted the church from moral standards applicable to the rest of society! Given the weak position of the church in British society -- only 3.8% of the population are on the electoral roll in any parish, and less than 3% indicate that they usually attend church on Sundays -- it is difficult to see how such legislation could avoid reinforcing the cynicism that much of the population apparently holds for the church as it is.

It was during the late 1960's and early '70's that the shift in sex roles in the larger society began to spill over into the churches. The discrepancies between concepts of justice and equality on the one hand and structural realities in the churches on the other became so apparent that the issue of women's role in the church was introduced as a formal item of discussion in the General Synod of the Church of England. The debate commenced in 1972, and in 1975 it ended temporarily with a vote in opposition to the ordination of women to Holy Orders.

Once the issue became formalized as a legitimate question for the church, the forces pressing for change broadened their base of support in the church, developed formal organizations for development and implementation of strategies, and gained more momentum. The 1978 bishops' conference effectively endorsed the ordination of women to the priesthood, but in the face of the debate between various segments of the Anglican communion, they equivocated and pleaded for tolerance and unity among the churches. But by this time the floodgates were open, and those seeking change increased their pressure on various church structures to endorse women's ordination.

Creation of "The Movement for the Ordination of Women"

An important organizational strategy which followed the 1978 Lambeth bishops' conference was the creation of the "Movement for the Ordination of Women" (MOW). The MOW was founded in July, 1979, with the express goal reflected in its title. The most direct impetus for the movement was the defeat in the House of Clergy of a motion endorsing the ordination of women. By 1986 MOW membership had reached about 3,500, and they had chapters all over England. They enjoyed increasing support among the Bishops, the laity, and even the clergy (who had been the most resistant in the procedings of the General Synod). A subgroup of clergy created their own organization in support of the MOW agenda, making public statements and chipping away at the resistance of other clergy and laity.

However, the opposition to the ordination of women in the Church of England was also organized. A group of MOW opponents created the group called "The Fellowship of Concerned Anglicans." The agenda of this body, of course, was to counter MOW campaigns with their own propaganda and parliamentary maneuvering and to prevent approval of the ordination of women by the General Synod. As of 1986 these opponents of women's ordination appeared to have been less successful than MOW, for the proportions of people endorsing the ordination of women had gradually increased more than those opposing the idea.

A report by Christian Howard (1984) illustrates the ways in which the pressures for change in sex roles in British society during this period influenced similar thrusts within the church. She writes, "there is no doubt that the church-wide debate from 1972-1975 and the return of the issue in 1978 raised many hopes..." (1984: 29). Increasing numbers of women perceived the possibility of pursuing more significant roles in the churches, and they began to act to realize those aspirations.

Several statistics cited by Howard (1984: 23-30) reflect these trends. There had been a clear rise in the number of women presenting themselves as candidates for the ministry, and those women appeared to have more intellectual ability and other pertinent skills than their male counterparts. In 1973 there were but forty-five women attending ministerial selection conferences. By 1983 this number had increased almost four-fold to 175 female conferees. The number of women in training for "accredited lay ministry" rose in similar fashion -- from 58 in 1973 to 218 in 1983. And there was a corresponding rise in the number of ordinations as deaconess, going from 81 in 1969 to 312 in 1983. Many of these women becoming deaconesses viewed the step as a "way station" en route to eventual ordination as priests once the rules of the game were changed. During this period, there was also a significant increase in the number of _married_ women offering for the ministry. Finally, the number of women registered as Readers in the church increased from 9 in 1969 to nearly 1100 in 1986.

Howard also points out that "a call for a real women's ministry, when translated into practical terms, often turns out to be no more than women _already_ do in the

Church of England today" (emphasis in the original; 1984: 30). As of 1982 there were about 333 women already "fully trained to the requirements for ordinands..." (1984: 28).

The Church of Scotland manifested some "one-upmanship" during this period by endorsing the ordination of women. There were 50 women ministers in that body in 1983, and 39 of those clergywomen were serving in parishes. At that time there were also 15 women probationers and 23 women in training. Women clergy in 1984 constituted about 3% of those already serving in the ministry. But women comprised about 13% of the candidates in training, so their proportional numbers were likely to increase gradually from that point forward.

Women Ordained Overseas

The early 1980's saw a great intensification of the debate within the Church of England, due at least in part to the activities of MOW. The women-in-ministry forces made gains in some quarters but encountered losses in others. One issue on which the conservative forces prevailed dealt with denominational endorsement of the ordination of women in other sections of the "Anglican Communion," i.e. women in denominations related to the Church of England but in other countries, such as Episcopalians in the United States. The General Synod would not endorse the concept of honoring the ordination of these women to allow them to carry out their ministry when in English parishes. The bulk of the resistance to the idea resided in the House of Clergy, which failed to give the measure the required two-thirds majority vote. The Houses of Bishops and of Laity were more inclined to approve of the measure. In 1986 majorities of all three houses endorsed the idea, but the motion failed to get the

required two-thirds majority in the Houses of Clergy and
of Laity.

Women's Ordination at Home

A major victory for the MOW forces came in the
autumn of 1984 when the direct issue of women's ordination
to the priesthood was given preliminary consideration. On
November 15, 1984, the Synod passed a motion "to bring
forward legislation to permit the ordination of women to
the priesthood..." (MOW, 1985: 8). A national opinion
poll just prior to the synod (N=2000) revealed that about
79% of the public and fully 84% of church members were in
favor of women's ordination (MOW, 1985). Among those
church members who attend church services at least once a
week, the level of approval was 66%. The rate of
endorsement was 80% among members who attend church at
least once a month. Once again the Synod vote represented
a preliminary skirmish. Nevertheless, the outcome also
indicated the continued drift of opinion in the direction
of endorsement of women in ministry. In July, 1986, the
Bishops assumed responsibility for moving the issue
forward to endorsement. The proponents of women's
ordination had reason to be cautiously optimistic.

Ordination of Women as Deacons

The forces of change were also successful in relation
to the ordination of women as deacons. This measure
passed the crucial vote in General Synod on July 2, 1985,
and again on July 7, 1986, endorsing the concept of women
as ordained deacons. This change was significant in that
previously the Order of Deacons had been reserved for men,
and the position was assumed to be something of an

apprenticeship to the priesthood. Thus to open the diaconate to women was perceived by most observers as another step toward the eventual ordination of women to that key position. Once passed in the General Synod, the measure went to Parliament which must approve any major changes in the Church of England.

The forces both pro and con correctly saw the step as a foot in the door of ordination to Holy Orders. Perhaps the key to its eventual passage at that time resided in the elections to the next General Synod. The members of the Houses of Laity and Clergy stand for election every three years, and the time for the next round of elections was at hand. The new delegates of the laity and clergy would be the ones to take up the measure when it came up for final vote in the next General Synod.

OTHER DENOMINATIONS

The impact of challenges to traditional sex roles in the church has also been felt in the Roman Catholic Church in England. This influence is apparent in the establishment of "St. Joan's Alliance," a Catholic women's organization devoted to equal rights for women. The organization was founded in 1911 in England. The initial focus of the Alliance was on women's suffrage, prostitution, child abuse, and other family issues. The founders took Joan of Arc as their patron saint. They received little recognition at first, but eventually they spread to other nations and stabilized a membership in Britain. At the outset St. Joan's published a periodical called The Catholic Suffragist, and they later changed the title to The Catholic Citizen. They also broadened their agenda to include the ordination of women to the priesthood in the Catholic Church.

St. Joan's Alliance may have had some impact on British Catholics. In 1973 there was a survey of Roman Catholic laypersons in England belonging to Newman Circles, family group organizations, and Catholic women's groups. The study was done by the Newman Association Family Committee. They surveyed a national sample of 275 persons. The general patterns in the responses indicated that lay members perceived sex discrimination in the Church. The results also revealed that most of the respondents favored the ordination of women as priests, although there was also evidence of polarization on that issue (SMWC: 1981).

INTERDENOMINATIONAL LINKAGES

It would be a mistake to assume that the women-in-ministry movement was restricted to a few denominations in the United States and Britain. It in fact involved most large western (Judaeo-Christian) societies and European communities in other parts of the world. The interdenominational nature of the movement to enhance the role of women in the church was reflected in several formal organizations. The issue of the role of women in the Church had been systematically incorporated in the agenda of the World Council of Churches, such as in the work of the Department on the Cooperation of Men and Women in Church, Family and Society. In the United States, the National Council of Churches established the Commission on Women in Ministry to promote the interests of women seeking to expand their involvements in the life of the churches.

In England the interdenominational character of the women-in-ministry movement was best reflected in the Society for the Ministry of Women in the Church (SMWC).

The SMWC was founded just after World War I, a period when women had just assumed responsibility for the pulpits in many locations due to the absence of clergymen who were away in the military. At this time a few religious bodies had ordained some women, but they had to deal with a great deal of prejudice. Women were not allowed to attend theological colleges, but instead had to go to separate training schools.

The SMWC came into being largely through the work of Maude Royden (SMWC, 1981; 1983), who was born to affluent parents November 23, 1876, near Liverpool. Always a precocious being, Ms. Royden excelled academically and completed a degree at Oxford University in 1899. After some disillusionment with her first job at a women's settlement house in Liverpool, she joined the women's suffrage movement in 1908. She experienced instant success as a speaker and leader in that context, and she concentrated her efforts more and more on improving the role of women in the church.

In 1917 Maude became disillusioned with the Church of England, which had continuously opposed her efforts at reform, and she became pastor of a Congregational church in London. She then left the post after six years to establish an interdenominational chapel in London where her worship services routinely attracted large crowds. (She was in and out of conflict with the Bishop of London for her occasional "irregular" services held in Anglican parishes.)

In 1929 Royden and a few colleagues organized a group to promote the interests of women in the churches. The first meeting took place in Central Hall, Westminster, on May 3, 1929. The hall was packed. The meeting established the Society for the Ministry of Women in the Church and set up an interdenominational steering committee. Maude Royden was elected the first President. Most subsequent meetings centered in London, although the organization spread to other cities and made contacts with persons on the Continent and in America.

Maude Royden worked with and through the SMWC until her death in 1956. By that time her insight and work enjoyed wide recognition. She was awarded the Ll.D. degree from Liverpool University in 1925. In 1939 she became the first woman in Britain to receive the Doctor of Divinity degree, awarded by Glasgow University. She was a popular lecturer, usually surprising her audiences with the powerful and persuasive style to come from her diminutive frame. Late in life she conducted a weekly radio broadcast which also enjoyed considerable popularity.

The SMWC was still in existence in 1986, pressing for a variety of social reforms both inside and outside of the churches including, of course, the ordination of women. They held annual meetings, usually in London, and they maintained their interdenominational membership which included persons from the Roman Catholic community. They published a periodical newsletter covering women's issues in churches all over the world. Even though their active participants tended to be older than those active in MOW, they nevertheless remained an important link between feminist forces in various religious bodies.

Summary

The pressures exerted by women in various parts of the world to enter the ranks of ordained clergy are in part a manifestation of a modern, secularized form of consciousness. The key characteristics of this mode of awareness are its tendencies to question traditional social and cultural patterns and to view them instead in historical and relativistic terms -- as products of human inventiveness which are neither sacred nor exempt from efforts to bring them in line with contemporary value orientations. As people have appropriated this perspective on society, they have wrought numerous transformations of basic social institutions -- the economy, politics, medicine, education, leisure, etc.

This book examines a movement to modify traditional sex roles in one social institution, i.e. organized religion. The work reports the results of a study of lay church members' responses to the movement to ordain women as clergy. The movement itself reflects the impact of secularizing forces. Each time members of the churches participating in the study considered the women-in-ministry issue, their actions had been preceded by changes in sex roles in society outside of the churches. Those secular alterations in gender-specific expectations for behavior appear to have constituted an important impetus for challenging traditional sex roles in the churches. The transformation of consciousness of who men and women are and what they are expected or allowed to do began in secular society and then spilled over into religious institutions. In this sense the women-in-ministry movement itself is a "modernizing" and "secularizing" phenomenon.

THINGS TO COME

The remainder of the book reports the results of the empirical study of attitudes toward clergywomen in England. In chapter 2 we shall review the rationale and basic structure of the research -- the specific conceptualizations of the issues, the characteristics of the national sample of church members, and the ways in which we measured differences in receptivity to women clergy and other variables. This section constitutes a basic description of the orientations of English church members to the concept of women as ministers.

The next three chapters involve a shift away from a descriptive approach to an explanatory one. Given the apparent differences in the way lay church members deal with women-in-ministry issues, how can we account for those variations in attitude? Chapter 3 examines the effects of background characteristics and finds some support for the notion that the secularization thesis also accounts for some of the attitudinal differences. The more lay members manifested characteristics associated with modern consciousness, the more they also tended to endorse the concept of women as ordained clergy. The chapter also demonstrates the effects of variations in individual religious commitment.

The fourth chapter examines the effect of differences in local/cosmopolitan orientation on religious sexism. It sets forth different ways of conceiving of "localism" and demonstrates that some of these perspectives are predictive of varying levels of receptivity to women clergy. These patterns also have relevance for the modern consciousness thesis.

Chapter 5 moves from the individual level of analysis to the level of organized groups -- the denominations and the local congregations. The analysis shows clearly that denominational differences are important in dealing with acceptance/rejection of women clergy. There is also evidence that the type of local congregation in which the member participates creates a background against which the women-in-ministry issue is judged.

The analysis in chapter 6 shows that some of the resistance to women ministers is organizational in nature, i.e. as members perceive (correctly or incorrectly) that the introduction of women clergy into the life of the congregation will threaten the organizational viability of the group through conflict and schism, the level of acceptance of women in ministry declines.

In chapter 7 the analysis turns international. Many of the measures employed in the study were also used in similar research in the United States. This practice allows us to make direct comparisons of lay attitudes in the United States and the United Kingdom. The results show both similarities and differences between the two societies, some of which are predictable while others are somewhat unexpected.

The final chapter is devoted to a multivariate analysis in which all types of variables are introduced into an analysis of differences in religious sexism. This step serves to show which factors are the more predictive of variations in receptivity to clergywomen. The section also produces a series of "composite portraits" of persons for and against the ordination of women. The chapter ends with a review of the major conclusions to derive from the study, along with an attempt to plumb their implications.

CHAPTER 2
CHURCH MEMBERS' ATTITUDES

The developments summarized in Chapter One show several instances of the churches being influenced by a peculiar orientation to social institutions that comes with modern consciousness, a questioning of traditional sex roles. One focus of much of this challenge is the ordination of women as clergy. A few denominations have been secularized, endorsing the ordination of women, and with that move a growing number of congregations have experienced females in the role of minister. Other religious bodies have clung to tradition, with the result that women were still barred from ordination as of 1986, as in the case of the Church of England.

While obtaining denominational endorsement amounts to an important step in the process of integrating women into the ranks of the clergy, such pronouncements at the denominational level do not remove all of the barriers. It would be a mistake to assume that lay church members in a given denomination are all of the same mind on this issue (or any other, for that matter). It also does not follow that just because denominational spokesmen articulate a policy position on an issue, the lay members will fall in line with the group's official stance. It simply does not work that way. Previous research on church members' attitudes towards women in ministry in the United States suggests that denominational pronouncements are not very good predictors of church members' individual attitudes (see, for example, Lehman, 1981a; 1985; and Carroll, et al, 1983). Even in churches where women's ordination has been approved, some laypersons still oppose the concept both as individuals and as congregations. It works the other way too. Sometimes lay members are more progressive than the clergy. As shown in Chapter One above, even though the Anglican Church had not endorsed women's entry into Holy Orders by 1984, in that year about four-fifths of Anglicans nation-wide said they approved the ordination of women. Official policy does not automatically determine the orientations of persons in the pews.

This is especially likely to be the case where the issue in dispute involves major departures from tradition. The application of modern consciousness to sex roles has always been accompanied by some controversy. While some denominational leaders come to view the ministry in non-traditional terms, it may be more difficult for other members with more parochial perspectives on the issue to adopt the same way of looking at it.

To persons directly involved in the controversy over the role of women in the churches, the critical questions are theological and ethical ones. Is the present posture right? Ought women to be ordained? Is there an unambiguous Biblical principle involved? Does the ordination of women violate fundamental theological principles. Can continued exclusion of women from the ministry be justified on moral grounds? Should churches make so radical a departure from tradition? Issues like these have been the focus of most of the literature associated with the women-in-ministry question in Britain up to now.

A Sociological Approach

In this undertaking, the approach was sociological rather than theological or ethical. Instead of joining the debate, this investigation sought to stand outside of it in order to gain a different perspective on what has been taking place. We wanted to shed some light where there had been mostly heat. The goals were similar to those involved in other sociological work, i.e. to describe and explain. Descriptively we wanted to portray several aspects of how English lay church members were reacting to the concept of women clergy. What was involved? As for explanation, we sought to explore possible reasons why church members dealt with the issue differently. Why did some members approve while others did not? So instead of examining the issue in terms of a set of ethical ideals or a system of theological discourse, we endeavored simply to ask what in fact was going on and why.

It is my hope that a report of an empirical analysis can serve as an antidote to one of our favorite human foibles, i.e. overgeneralizing from a narrow base of information. We are all guilty from time to time of describing "what everybody thinks" about various issues, "what everyone likes" about them, and "what everybody really needs." Especially in matters where we have some vested interest, there are at least two fallacies involved in such activity: overgeneralizing from a few specifics with which we happen to be familiar but which are but a small part of the total picture, and then drawing normative implications which do not necessarily follow, but instead reflect our own preferences in the situation.

Thus the value of a study such as this often resides in its calling "a pox on both your houses!" It presents a reality check to persons representing both sides of an issue, correcting some of their biased perceptions and explanations, and providing ground for more common understanding and future cooperation. Those outcomes are possible where people give facts higher priority than personal opinion, even though the realities may be different from what they would like to see from their theological perspective. This book will have been worth the trouble if, in addition to supplementing our general knowledge of the interface between religion and society, it can also serve to move the discussion in that direction.

A NATIONAL SURVEY

In any case, the pressures to modify traditional sex roles in the churches in England are clearly manifest. At the denominational level, some groups have modified their concepts of ministry to allow for women's ordination, and others have not. What do the lay members think about it? We went to them to ask them directly.

During the first quarter of 1984, we conducted a survey of a national sample of lay church members in four denominations in England -- the Church of England, the Baptist Union, the Methodist Church, and the United Reformed Church. These denominations were selected because they represented major Protestant bodies in England and because they would yield data that would allow direct comparisons between the English data and parallel information obtained from similar denominations in the United States. We chose not to include Roman Catholics, Jewish congregations, or members of smaller sects simply because of limited resources and because we did not have similar data from such groups in the United States. One cannot study everything on a finite budget, so we chose those groups which would allow direct extensions of other work already completed elsewhere.

Sampling

We selected a sampling plan which would give us information from church members who were representative of the entire population of such people. In technical terms, it was a stratified multi-stage cluster sample. Using directories obtained from denominational offices, we identified an equal number of parishes or congregations in each denomination in the three major culture areas of the country, i.e. the North, the Midlands, and the South. The division between North and Midlands was a line running roughly from Grimsby to Leeds and then on to Liverpool. The dividing line between Midlands and South ran approximately from King's Lynn to Bristol.

The goal was to obtain a sample of about 400 lay church members in each denomination. Within each religious body, we drew a systematic sample of 27 parishes or congregations in each of the three regions. This information was available directly from the denominational directories of the Baptist Union, the Methodist Church, and the United Reformed Church. In the case of the Church of England, we obtained the list of parishes with the help of the offices of the dioceses included in the sample. We then telephoned the minister or priest of each congregation to obtain the names of five church members according to the following criteria:

1. take the first five names alphabetically, except:
2. no one under age 18,
3. no one infirm or chronically ill, and
4. only one person per nuclear family; if a male is included from one family, select the female from the next one, etc.

Following this routine, we hoped to obtain an unbiased national sample of adult lay church members in the four denominations.

The overall level of cooperation was very high. Over 95 per cent of the pastors and vicars cooperated and supplied lists of members as specified. (The one likely exception to this response was reflected in the list we obtained from an Anglican vicar. It included the names of a Baroness, a military Squadron Leader, a Member of Parliament, a physician, and another person of noteworthy status. This sample might have happened by chance, but it does stretch one's credulity just a bit!) The clergy who supplied such lists of parishioners also completed a short questionnaire used to obtain information about some basic characteristics of their congregation -- size, type of community, budget, etc.

Data Collection

The data-collection process involved a mailed questionnaire. The mailing packet included the form, a cover letter explaining the purpose of the study and inviting respondents to phone the investigator reverse-charge if they had questions, and a self-addressed stamped envelope for use in returning the completed questionnaire. In the case of members of Baptist, Methodist, and United Reformed Churches, the mailing also included a letter of endorsement from the denominational offices in London. It was not possible to obtain such assistance from officials of the Church of England. The total data-collection phase proceeded in three stages, i.e. an initial complete mailing, a post-card follow-up after two weeks, and another complete mailing to non-respondents after another two weeks.

The level of cooperation among the lay church members was almost as high as that obtained from the pastors. As shown in Table 2.1, the overall response rate to the lay survey was about 91 per cent. Members of the United Reformed Church gave the highest level of cooperation as reflected in their response rate of 95 per cent. The Anglican church members were lowest at 87 per cent. The table also shows the regional distribution of the total eventual sample -- very close to the trichotomized goal.

All told we can place considerable confidence in the representativeness of the sample which was ultimately drawn. This judgement was reinforced by some cross-checks of sample characteristics with known population parameters in one denomination, the results of which showed the traits of the sample to resemble known membership figures quite closely.

ATTITUDES TOWARDS WOMEN IN MINISTRY

To ask about church members' responses to the idea of women as ordained clergy is to inquire about their attitudes. Attitude research has a long and complicated history in social psychology (see, for example, Allport, 1958; and Petty and Cacioppo, 1981). It will serve little purpose to review that field here. Instead we shall simply stipulate how the concept of "attitude" is defined in this work, and if readers wish to take exception to that usage so be it. At least our usage will be known.

Attitudes lay behind many of our actions towards other people and other objects around us. We prefer to act in one way towards other people if we like them and in quite different ways if we do not. This business of liking and disliking something, being disposed to act favorably or unfavorably towards things, is largely what we mean by "attitudes."

This is not to argue that people are always consistent -- that we consistently act out our attitudes. Sometimes there are situational constraints that do not allow us to put our ideas and feelings into overt action. At times these external realities pattern what we do in

TABLE 2.1   SAMPLE SIZE AND RATE OF RESPONSE FROM A SURVEY OF LAY CHURCH MEMBERS IN FOUR DENOMINATIONS IN ENGLAND

Denomination	Target Sample	Number of Returns	Percent
Church of England	400	347	87
Baptist Union	392	360	92
Methodist Church	390	349	89
United Reformed Church	375	358	95
TOTAL	1557	1414	91

Regional distribution of sample (percent):

North	32
Midlands	35
South	33

spite of our attitudes. For example, we may prefer to discriminate against a member of some minority group, but the law or a set of organizational policies prohibit such moves, or we might want to hire a member of our family to fill a position in the firm we work for, but company policies against nepotism prevent it.

However, there is also much to be said for the idea that our attitudes are always there, operating in the background and motivating us to want to act in particular ways towards people and other attitude objects around us. The person who is prejudiced (an attitude) against black people, for example, would be motivated to act negatively toward a black person regardless of the situation of the moment. In the absence of contextual restraints, that person would carry his/her attitudes into overt actions.

So if we want some idea of the way in which people are likely to act towards some object of interest -- be that object another person, an inanimate object such as money, or an intangible object such as a policy or a law- - it is useful to know their attitudes towards that object. In this case we are interested in knowing what kind of responses we can expect from church members dealing with the idea of women in ministry. It will be helpful to know their attitudes towards women clergy.

Dimensions of Attitudes

The concept of attitudes summarizes a complex set of interrelated long-term characteristics of individuals. For most social psychologists working with the concept, it has become useful to think of them in terms of three dimensions. These three facets of attitudes center on human capacities for thinking, feeling, and acting.

The thinking dimension:

The "thinking" dimension -- sometimes also called the "cognitive" or "perceptual" dimension -- amounts to an individual's conceptual understanding of what the attitude object is like. It is reflected, for example, in the description one would expect from an Anglican resident of London listing the characteristics of an Irish Catholic. It is seen in how a young person is likely to describe an "old woman" and how a middle-class small-town butcher might describe a "city woman on public assistance." It is also reflected, of course, in this writer's attributions to persons listed above as "Anglican Londoners," "young persons," and "middle-class small-town butchers."

This dimension of attitudes is most clearly related to the way in which most of us have been taught to think of "prejudice" -- to prejudge -- to think of a member of some group (or other category of objects) in terms of an image we have in mind ahead of time and which we superimpose on that person. This mode of thinking becomes "prejudice" when that a priori judgement is inaccurate, unfair, or somehow injurious to the person about whom we are thinking or talking. It is usually especially frowned upon when it also leads to actions that are considered discriminatory.

Equally importantly, it would be a mistake to deal with the perceptual dimension of attitudes only in negative terms or with the assumption that the thought involved is intrinsically inaccurate. Our perceptions may deal with the object in very positive ways. For instance, we also have preconceived ideas of members of groups we like, as in typical assumptions about our family, the group with whom we work, our favorite football team, or the musical group we like best. Just as negative prejudice may have little to do with the actual characteristics of the attitude object, so these positive assumptions may not resemble reality either.

Similarly, one's perception of an object may be quite accurate. A young person's description of an "old woman" can range from being "spot-on" to being so wide of the mark as to be completely false. Nevertheless, whether positive or negative, correct or incorrect, the thinking dimension constitutes an important element of the attitudes which lay behind our actions. It amounts to our assumptions about what the object is like, and it constitutes a basis for feelings of liking or disliking the object.

<u>We set out in the survey to learn what lay church members think clergywomen are like.</u> When religious devotees think of "ordained women clergy," what images come to their mind? To what extent do they view the objects "woman" and "ministry" in traditional terms? Conversely, to what degree are they able to depart from traditional role definitions and conceive of "woman ministers" in positive terms? We wanted to examine this perceptual dimension of church members' attitudes towards women in ministry empirically.

The feeling dimension:

While the cognitive dimension discussed above is what some would call "head stuff," i.e. a matter of what people think, the "feeling" dimension deals with "gut-level stuff" -- a matter of <u>affect</u>. It consists of what people like and dislike, attractions and aversions to this or that object. It deals with our feelings.

In relation to the concept of "prejudice" we used as an illustration above, the affective dimension is the point of reference for those who argue that prejudice is not a very rational thing. It is more of an emotional matter, i.e. antipathies. Feelings -- often raw emotions -- lay behind many of our actions toward others. They reflect the hatred, the love, the fascination, and the despair that motivates so many elements of human life.

Such feelings, along with the actions which flow from them, are often hard to explain. They seem so irrational at times, so hard to deal with logically. Many of our feelings simply do not make sense even to ourselves. We act out some of these things in ways which at times seem so illogical. "I don't know why I said that," we often confess, genuinely mystified by the apparent depth of an emotional push that results in actions clearly contrary to rational thought.

In the survey, we set out to learn the extent to which people like and dislike the idea of women in ministry. The depth of feeling often associated with remarks made in relation to this issue can be profound. I recall talking with a deaconess participating in her push for the ordination of women. Her whole face trembled as she recounted various experiences of rejection. "Why are they so threatened by us?" she asked. "How can they legitimately stand in the way of my doing something I know God wants me to do?" "How can the blatant misogyny of a few insecure priests who don't know how to respond to women be represented as God's will for the Church?"

The level of feeling appears to be no less intense among those who oppose the ordination of women. A priest got up to speak at a public forum set up to discuss the issue. "I have no objection to women engaging in many forms of ministry," he said. "But when you speak of the ordination of women, you are dealing with Holy Orders!" As he uttered the last two words, "Holy Orders," there was a profound depth of feeling reflected in his voice and on his face. It signified a sense of awe and reverence for that form of ministry that was unrivaled by any other station in life. To him the ordained priesthood was indeed a role set apart by God. It was also one with which one dare not tamper lightly. And this sense of the sacred also applied, in his opinion, to the norm specifying that the role is reserved to males to serve as the "Vicar" or representation of Christ to the world. To open it to women was a profound sacrilege to him.

The participants in the debate, usually clergy and a few laity involved in denominational affairs such as those in the Anglican House of Laity, include many individuals in whom the women-in-ministry issue arouses deep feelings both pro and con. But what about the ordinary person in the pew? How does the "average church member" feel about it? More accurately put, how do the many different kinds of "average church member" feel about the ordination of women? To what extent do they actively wish to retain only traditional sex roles in church leadership? How much are they open to experimentation in this arena -- willing to apply modern values in their corporate religious life? We sought to obtain some answers to those questions in the national survey.

The behavioral dimension:

The third dimension -- the "behavioral" -- simply refers to what we do overtly rather than what we think or feel. Recall our discussion above that we do not always act rationally, and we are similarly inconsistent in terms of acting out our feelings. The frequent discrepancies between "what we say and what we do" (e.g. Deutscher, 1973) are there for all to see.

If the thinking and feeling dimensions of a negative sort refer to what "prejudice" is all about, then the behavioral or overt action component of attitudes represents "discrimination." It is a matter of how we are motivated to behave toward the attitude object if we are to act out the implications of our perceptions and feelings. It is the behavioral dimension of attitudes that is reflected in the Montgomery, Alabama, bus driver's insistence that black persons sit at the rear of the coach. It is the hospital administrator's refusal to appoint the best qualified person as Chief of Surgery because she is a woman.

This action component of attitudes towards women in ministry, of course, has to be the "bottom line." When confronted with the choice of allowing women to function as clergy or not, individuals will either endorse the idea or they will oppose it. They may choose one course of action over another for a variety of reasons, and they may make their individual decisions lightly or only after considerable reflection. But they will in fact react one way or another.

For a few members, the response takes place in policy-making bodies, such as the Anglican General Synod, the Methodist Conference, or the annual Baptist convention of delegates. For most others, however, the overt response occurs in much less dramatic fashion. It is a vote for or against the ordination of women in a parish discussion. It is a vote for or against calling a woman as minister of the congregation in bodies where such decisions are made locally. It is a decision to remain in a congregation where a woman has been installed as pastor, or the opposite choice to leave. It is a decision whether or not to keep attending worship services where the minister is a woman, and a choice concerning ongoing financial contributions to the church. These are the actions in which most people engage concerning women in ministry. <u>In the survey we wanted to learn how church members were prepared to act toward women clergy.</u>

Normally these three dimensions of attitudes are interrelated. People will be more inclined to discriminate against members of some group (the behavioral dimension) if they also do not like the group (the feeling component), and they will feel such aversions toward that group if they also perceive negative traits in its members or the organization itself (the cognitive dimension). Most individuals normally function this way. However, it is also important to look first at each dimension separately so as to understand the patterns which emerge in each case. Then we can examine the possible interrelations between them. This is the way in which we shall approach the three dimensions in the analysis below.

MEASURING ATTITUDES TOWARDS CLERGYWOMEN

The survey questionnaire consisted of items designed to measure differences in attitudes towards women in ministry and other variables. The indicators of each dimension of lay attitudes towards women clergy consisted of the following sets of questions.

The Cognitive Dimension

One section of the form contained a series of statements designed to get at the variations in members' traditional/modern perceptions of clergywomen. The statements made various assertions about characteristics of women in ministry, and we asked the respondents to indicate whether they thought each one was true or false. This section of the form, along with the percentages of persons responding in each way, are contained in Table 2.2.

We chose to measure differences in the perceptual aspect of attitudes toward clergywomen in terms of a set of stereotypes imposed on women who seek to enter fields dominated by men. It seems that whenever women have tried to function in occupations -- especially professions -- to which men have had virtually exclusive access, those women have taken on predictable stereotyped images (see, for example, Epstein, 1970). The stereotypes portray women professionals as overly emotional in crisis situations, as unable to handle conflict competently, as unreliable on the job due to home responsibilities and the supposed debilitating effects of the menstrual cycle, etc. These ready-made attributes have been imposed on women entering medicine, law, corporate management, the military, etc. They represent traditional forms of thinking that function to allow people to resist modern, open definitions of sex roles. The goal here was to determine the extent to which those traditional stereotypes also befall women entering the ranks of the clergy. The patterns, then, also represent one way of assessing how lay church members think of women as ordained clergy.

There are several obvious patterns in the church members' responses to these items. First, there are wide differences in the extent to which people hold each stereotype listed. This indicates that we have indeed measured a "variable" and that church members are not monolithic on any facet of images of women in ministry. This pattern serves to warn us against making hasty generalizations about "how church members view women clergy." The picture is quite complicated, and facile portraits of "what everyone thinks" are clearly out of place.

Nevertheless, and secondly, within this variability it is also possible to discern tendencies for members' perceptions to go one way or the other depending on which stereotype is involved. On the negative side, the majority of respondents hold stereotyped perceptions of women's relative ability to manage the cross pressures of responsibilities at home and on the job. Nearly three-fourths expect these conflicts to give the woman minister emotional problems. A similar pattern exists concerning women's ability to handle the sexist language issue. Two thirds of the respondents assume that dealing with that issue will result in alienation of the clergywoman from her congregation.

On the majority of the items, however, most church members do not manifest the stereotyped responses to the questions. They do _not_ tend to view women clergy as persons who will be undependable on the job, as unable to nurture their children adequately, or as otherwise temperamentally unsuited for the work of the ministry. The prevailing perceptions of these characteristics of clergywomen are positive.

The patterns of response to the remaining items in the table show that members tend to be equally divided on the question of whether women are relatively strong or weak leaders and whether or not being divorced would uniquely interfere with the woman's effectiveness as a minister.

These variations in church members' perceptions of women clergy are noteworthy for several reasons, not the least of which is the fact that they exist largely in the absence of any systematic interaction with clergywomen. Very few of the members had experienced the pastoral leadership of a woman. Few had even known a woman minister. Yet they are able to indicate whether or not a

TABLE 2.2   PATTERNS OF STEREOTYPING WOMEN IN MINISTRY AMONG PROTESTANT
LAY CHURCH MEMBERS IN ENGLAND (PERCENT)

"The following list of statements represents a variety of opinions some persons have about women in the ministry. We would like to know what you think about each one. After you read each statement, please 'tick' the appropriate column beside it to indicate whether you think the statement is 'definitely true', 'probably true', 'probably false', or 'definitely false'.

THERE ARE NO 'RIGHT' OR 'WRONG' ANSWERS.   Forget what others may think. It is YOUR opinions we need."

	definitely true	probably true	probably false	definitely false
*A woman minister who is married can fulfill her responsibilities as wife and mother just as well as if she were not working full-time.	14	42	25	19
Women ministers are likely to have higher levels of absenteeism from work than men.	6	33	38	23
Women ministers are likely to change pastorates more often than are men.	2	16	53	30

TABLE 2.2 (continued)

Being divorced would impair the ministry of a woman more than of a man.	13	31	28	29
Women who try to be both full-time ministers and also wives and mothers are likely to have emotional problems due to all the demands placed on them.	20	51	22	8
The children of women who are full-time ministers are likely to have personal problems due to lack of care and attention.	7	29	39	26
Most churches today need the strong leadership that a man is better able to give.	21	25	24	30
* A woman's temperament is just as suited for the pastoral ministry as is a man's.	45	38	11	6
A woman minister who openly questions the traditional male language about God will alienate many members of her church.	20	46	28	6

* Persons disagreeing with this question manifest the stereotyped response.
  Persons agreeing with the other items manifest the stereotyped response.

variety of specific characteristics legitimately apply to women as clergy. Since the source of the images is not the attitude object itself, the perceptions must derive from some other source, quite probably the individual members' applications of traditional cultural roles of women to the concept of ministry. Some members have difficulty with this interface of roles not traditionally experienced together, while others seem to have few problems with the possible new forms. (We shall return to the question of whether contact with clergywomen affects these perceptions in another stage of the analysis below.)

Sub-dimensions of stereotyping:

The next question we asked about church members' perceptions of women in ministry was whether these laypersons dealt with each statement in Table 2.2 as a unique issue, or instead as sets of items grouped together in their mind on the basis of some underlying criteria. Did they respond to the questions as unrelated to each other, or did they answer them as subsets of items having implicit themes in common?

To answer this query, we subjected the responses to the statements in Table 2.2 to a "factor analysis." Factor analysis compares the way the respondents answered each question to their replies to all other questions. The result indicates the extent to which answering one item is correlated with responses to others. The technique yields groupings of items which appear to "factor" (cluster) together based on the patterns of actual response. By examining the content of questions whose answers appear highly correlated, each cluster being called a "factor," one can often infer the underlying criteria by which people dealt with items in each subset.

The results of this factor analysis are contained in Table 2.3, where one sees evidence that the members tended to deal with the stereotyping items in two groupings. The coefficients indicate two subsets of four items each. Within each subset the replies to the questions are correlated, and these internal intercorrelations are greater than relationships between the two clusters.

This pattern implies that the church members answered one set of perceptual items according to one criterion, and that they dealt with the other cluster in terms of another criterion. The concept implicit in the first factor deals mainly with the extent to which women are capable of handling the cross-pressures of home and job. People who thought women could not simultaneously handle responsibilities in both places also thought the women would have emotional problems, that their children would be disturbed, and that the problem was simply that women are temperamentally less well suited for the ministry than are men.

The concept underlying the second factor, on the other hand, was a matter of general dependability on the job. Members who thought that women could not provide as strong pastoral leadership as men also tended to think women would manifest high levels of absenteeism and high rates of job turnover, and that if the clergywomen were divorced it would jeopardize their work more than if they were men.

So the results of the factor analysis suggest that the members tended not to deal with the perceptual questions in isolation from each other. Instead they replied in terms of at least two general criteria, two broad areas of concern imbedded in the stereotypes -- an issue of possible role conflict involving demands of job and home, and a second issue of general reliability as

Table 2.3

DIMENSIONS OF STEREOTYPING WOMEN IN MINISTRY
AS DETERMINED BY FACTOR ANALYSIS

	Factor 1	Factor 2
A woman minister who is married can fulfill her responsibilities as wife and mother just as well as if she were not working full-time.	-.84	.00*
The children of women who are full-time ministers are likely to have personal problems due to lack of care and attention.	.71	.31
Women who try to be both full-time ministers and also wives and mothers are likely to have emotional problems due to all the demands placed on them.	.66	.34
A woman's temperament is just as suited for the pastoral ministry as is a man's.	-.61	.00*
Being divorced would impair the ministry of a woman more than of a man.	.00*	.77
Women ministers are likely to change pastorates more often than are men.	.00*	.74
Most churches today need the strong leadership that a man is better able to give.	.50	.59
Women ministers are likely to have higher levels of absenteeism from work than men.	.36	.53

* Coefficient less than criterion value of .30.

professional church workers. (The question dealing with the issue of sexist language did not cluster with either of these subsets. We shall return to the language issue in another phase of the analysis below.)

Composite indexes of stereotyping

For the sake of parsimony, in subsequent analyses of the "thinking component" of attitude towards women clergy, we shall deal with the variable in terms of these overall sub-dimensions. Instead of using each perceptual question alone, we shall use the combinations of items which clustered in each factor. We shall talk in terms of "role conflict stereotyping" and of "reliability stereotyping."

To facilitate this approach, we combined the two sets of items into two indexes -- a "role-conflict stereotyping index" and a "reliability stereotyping index." The role-conflict stereotyping index uses answers to the four items which loaded on the first factor, and the reliability stereotyping index incorporates the replies to the other four questions. Each index was constructed by simply giving each respondent a "score" based on the number of times he/she gave the stereotyped answer to a question in the set. A member received one point for each stereotyped response. Thus each person has a score ranging from "zero" for giving the stereotyped reply to none of the items to "four" for having answered all four questions in the stereotyped form. (We used the midpoint between "true" and "false" as the cutting point in scoring.) Thus each member in the survey received a "role conflict stereotyping score" and a "reliability stereotyping score" for use in later stages of the analysis where we compare differences in stereotyping propensities with other variables in an effort to account for attitudinal disparities.

The distributions of the scores on these two indexes are contained in Table 2.4. The assumption underlying each of these indexes is that the more items in each subset the person answers in the stereotyped way, the more that person tends to perceive women in ministry in stereotyped terms on that dimension. Persons with a score of "4," for example, gave the stereotyped response to all four items and is presumed to show a maximum tendency to stereotype clergywomen on that criterion. Those with a score of "0" indicate the minimum tendency to stereotype.

The distributions of scores in Table 2.4 represent another way of indicating the extent to which people view women in ministry in stereotyped terms. The general tendency on both indexes is clearly in the direction of little stereotyping. As indications of the prevalence of stereotypes among lay church members, the figures suggest that it is only a minority of church members who tend to

TABLE 2.4 DISTRIBUTIONS OF SCORES ON THE STEREOTYPING INDEXES AMONG
PROTESTANT LAY CHURCH MEMBERS IN ENGLAND

	low stereotyping			high stereotyping	
reliability score	0	1	2	3	4
percent	28	29	22	13	8

mean score = 1.44

	low stereotyping			high stereotyping	
role conflict score	0	1	2	3	4
percent	21	27	24	19	9

mean score = 1.67

view women in ministry in jaundiced terms. Most members appear to have more open perceptions of women clergy.

Note, secondly, that the differences between the distributions are not great. There is a slight tendency for more stereotyping on the criterion of "role conflict" than in terms of "reliability." The median score for the role conflict images is "2," while the median of the reliability scores is "1." This pattern implies that if there is any tendency for English church members to have reservations about specific characteristics of clergywomen, those hesitancies take the form of concerns about women's ability to meet conflicting demands of home and job more often than reservations about their general ability to function dependably as church workers. This pattern may be a function of other stereotyped sex roles which the respondents harbor, e.g. the relative roles of men and women within the family itself. It would seem that concerns over handling role conflict would have to be based on an assumption that domestic chores would remain the responsibility of the woman instead of the man. If this is the case, then we have another instance in which one stereotype tends to feed upon and support another (see also Nason-Clark, 1985). Such perceptions would also have to assume the absence of other support structures such as day-care facilities, domestic help, etc., arrangements that are actually rather common these days.

Summary:

In summary, then, these patterns are consistent with the following generalizations:

1. English church members differed widely in the extent to which they view women clergy in traditional stereotyped terms.

2. The members' responses to this particular set of items tended to correlate in such a way as to indicate two underlying dimensions of stereotyping. One form deals with whether or not women clergy will be generally reliable on the job. The other type focuses on whether women can handle the conflicting demands of job and home.

3. The general tendency among church members was to hold relatively few stereotypes of clergywomen. The majority of members tended to look upon women in ministry in relatively open and flexible terms. This suggests that most lay members are quite capable of departing from traditional conceptualizations of "women" and of "ministry." The application of a form of modern consciousness to matters of church leadership is not really a problem for them. These tendencies should bode well for the future acceptance of women in ministry.

The Feeling Dimension

The questionnaire also contained a series of questions designed to indicate the ways in which lay church members have feelings of attraction or aversion to the "modern" idea of women in leadership positions in the church. As shown in Table 2.5, these items were couched in terms of whether church members preferred a man, a woman, or had no preference in relation to a variety of church positions and ministerial activities. This issue of "wanting" a member of one sex or the other involves the affective component which differentiates the feeling dimension of attitudes from the cognitive component.

PATTERNS OF GENDER PREFERENCES FOR CLERGY ROLES AMONG PROTESTANT
LAY CHURCH MEMBERS IN ENGLAND (PERCENT)

	prefer a man (1)	no difference (2)	prefer a woman (3)
CHURCH POSITIONS			
senior or sole pastor	49	51	0
assistant pastor	21	73	6
denominational administrator	23	75	2
foreign missionary	14	79	7
college chaplain	43	56	1
PASTORAL ACTIVITIES			
performing a baptism	32	66	2
administering the Lord's Supper	31	68	1
preaching a sermon	21	78	1
conducting a funeral			
advising you about a personal problem	41	58	1
conducting a business meeting of the church	26	61	12
	27	72	1
guiding the church in a building programme	53	46	1
planning the congregation's annual budget	22	75	4
coordinate church staff as senior minister	36	62	1
perform a wedding	44	56	1
reading the scripture lesson during worship	5	92	3
leading a pastoral prayer	9	89	2

(Some terminology differed slightly from one denomination to another depending on the theological and organizational nomenclature involved. Except as noted elsewhere, however, the basic content of each item was the same for all four denominations.)

There are several patterns in the ways in which the members responded to the questions listed in the table. First, the basic distinction in most members' minds was between either preferring a man or having no preference for a male or female. Very few members indicated an explicit preference for a woman in any of the positions or activities. The major exception to this observation, of course, was the 12 per cent of respondents who indicated preference for a woman as the person to counsel them about a personal problem. This variance is explained easily in terms of the fact that most of those 12 per-cent are themselves women. So the basic tendency is for members either to prefer a man for this or that role or to have no gender preference at all.

The second pattern in the responses is that the majority of church members indicated "no preference" on all of the positions and activities but one. The tendency is clearly for most church members to be open to the idea of having either a man or a woman in these positions and performing these activities. Only on the issue of guiding the church in a building programme did more than 50 percent of members indicate a preference for a man. This divergence probably rests on a common assumption (perhaps misguided) that a man will automatically know more about constructing church buildings than a woman.

On the question of senior minister (or parish priest), the church members split nearly down the middle between those who prefer a man and those for whom gender would make no difference. The lowest proportion of members indicating preference for a male appeared on items dealing with reading scripture during worship and leading a pastoral prayer. This openness on these practices is probably an artifact of a fairly widespread custom of allowing laypersons, whether male or female, to perform these activities routinely. Also, few members indicated preference for a man as a foreign missionary. Evidently it is more acceptable to have a woman perform ministerial tasks overseas than at home.

Finally, it is noteworthy that even though members split evenly in gender preferences for the position of minister itself, an average of about two-thirds of them said that gender makes no difference concerning most activities ministers engage in for their parishioners. This pattern even applies to the issue of a person coordinating church staff as "senior minister." This discrepancy raises the question of why so many members would want a man in the position of minister when it makes no difference if a man or woman performs the tasks ministers typically do. Speculation might suggest that it is the symbolic vicarious or representational image of the position that these individuals want to retain in the hands of a male, while pragmatically it is immaterial that a woman may be able to do ministerial tasks as satisfactorily as one would normally expect of a man.

So, in spite of long-standing tradition, most members appear to be open to the idea of women occupying church positions of authority and performing most functions done by clergy. In this way there again appears to be more openness than closure to the involvement of women in the ordained ministry.

As we did with the stereotyping items, we wanted to find out whether subsets of these preference questions tended to cluster together in a way that would indicate sub-dimensions of gender preferences for clerical positions and activities. We subjected the patterns of

response to these questions to a factor analysis in order
to identify which subsets tended to be inter-correlated.
The results of the factor analysis are shown in Table
2.6. In this case the factor analysis produced four
separate dimensions of gender preferences in relation to
clergy roles. The first and clearest factor contains
items having in common a "liturgical" or "sacramental"
element. The positions of pastor, assistant pastor, and
college chaplain are clustered with activities of

TABLE 2.6 DIMENSIONS OF GENDER PREFERENCES FOR CLERGY ROLES AS
DETERMINED BY FACTOR ANALYSIS

	Factor 1	Factor 2	Factor 3	Factor 4
performing a wedding	.80	.21	.06	.07
administer Lord's Supper	.80	.18	.22	.02
conducting a funeral	.79	.22	.09	.10
performing baptism	.78	.16	.19	.04
senior or sole pastor	.67	.37	.07	-.03
assistant pastor	.54	.11	.39	.26
preaching a sermon	.45	.33	.44*	.11
college chaplain	.48	.42	.00	.18
planning the budget	.08	.70	.25	.11
guiding building programme	.19	.70	-.10	.07
conducting business meeting	.25	.66	.26	.10
coordinate church staff	.44	.64	.08	-.15
denominational administrator	.23	.46	.19	.18
read scripture lesson	.06	.10	.85	.07
lead pastoral prayer	.22	.14	.83	.02
foreign missionary	.01	.06	.02	.91
advise on personal problem	.23	.28	.23	.42

* also loads on factor #3.

administering Holy Communion, preaching sermons, performing baptism, and conducting funerals and weddings. Thus in most members' minds, it seems, gender preferences for clergy positions tend to be conceptualized largely in sacramental and liturgical terms.

The second factor indicates a subset of questions having very different underlying assumptions. The questions loading on the second factor are much more "organizational" than liturgical. They deal with the "nuts and bolts" of keeping a church organization alive and functioning. The fact that these questions loaded on a separate factor from the pastor item and the sacramental questions suggests that we have at least two criteria revealed in the church members' minds. Gender preferences for sacramental and liturgical matters are "one thing," but preferences for organizational concerns are "another thing."

The sets of items which comprised factors 3 and 4 in the factor analysis have already been dealt with above. Factor #3 contains those items in which laypersons have been involved for some years. Factor 4 is difficult to define, containing but two questions of rather diverse content. In any case, it is the first two factors which are likely to be important conceptually, and we shall concentrate on them (to the exclusion of the last two) in other analyses dealing with gender preferences below.

Indexes of Gender Preference:

As we did with the stereotyping items, we combined the questions comprising each factor on the "feeling" dimension to make four separate "indexes" to serve as composite indicators. Depending on how each member answered the questions in each subset, we calculated a score on each index to differentiate members in terms of the extent to which they had preferences for males in each kind of position and activity. This procedure yielded a range of "sacramental preferences scores," "organizational preferences scores," "lay liturgy preference scores," and (for lack of a better term) "subordinate preference scores."

The distributions of these scores are contained in Table 2.7. As appeared in the responses to the individual

Table 2.7

DISTRIBUTIONS OF SCORES ON THE GENDER-PREFERENCE INDEXES AMONG PROTESTANT LAY CHURCH MEMBERS IN ENGLAND

sacramental preference score*	0	1	2	3	4	5	6	7	8
percent	33	13	10	6	8	6	6	7	10

mean score = 5.22

organizational preference score*	0	1	2	3	4	5
percent	33	21	18	13	8	8

mean score = 3.36

lay liturgy preference score*	0	1	2	3
percent	77	15	4	4

mean score = 2.65

subordinate preference score*	0	1	2	3
percent	58	26	12	4

mean score = 2.39

* high score indicates maximum preference for males, and a low score indicates maximum openness to females.

items, in general the distributions of scores indicate considerable openness by church members to the idea of having women perform these functions. On the "sacramental score", only 10 per cent of members indicated a preference for a man on all 8 items in the sacramental index. Fully 33 per cent manifested preference for a man on none of them.

A similar pattern emerged on the distribution of "organizational" preference scores. And the distributions of the remaining two scores were even more highly skewed. These patterns reinforce the observations derived from Table 2.6, i.e. that there is widespread openness on the part of English church members to the idea of having women in clergy positions and performing clerical functions for their congregations.

Summary:

It seems safe to make the following generalizations about the characteristics of church members' feelings about clergywomen:

1. As was the case with perceptions of women in ministry, church members were not monolithic in terms of gender preferences for church positions and pastoral activities. On most functions and activities, significant proportions of the members disagreed over whether it is preferable to have a man in those roles.

2. Very few church members explicitly preferred a woman in these roles. The basic distinction in members' minds was between the traditional stance of preferring a man and the more modern orientation wherein gender made no difference to them.

3. Even though nearly half of the members preferred a man in the position of senior pastor or parish priest, only about half as many also preferred a man for most of the functions which those ministers perform. This inconsistency implies that it is not what clergy persons do that is of concern to many church members, but instead it is a matter of concern over who occupies the position itself. Perhaps there is simply something symbolic about the person behind the collar, a point which has been made by some opponents of the ordination of women.

4. Most of the preferences church members had concerning the gender of persons in clergy roles were based on two criteria. One underlying concern seems to be sacramental and liturgical. The gender of the incumbent of the ministerial position itself clustered on that dimension. The second criterion appears to be organizational. Concerns about who will keep the organizational machinery of the church running appear to be separate from liturgical issues in the minds of church members. Many of these patterns are similar to those observed in studies of receptivity to women in ministry in the United States (see Lehman, 1979; 1985).

THE BEHAVIORAL DIMENSION

We now come to the third dimension of attitudes--that associated with overt behavior. This is the "action" dimension. The focus here is on what lay church members were prepared to do in response to women in ministry. In the final analysis, would they accept or reject female clergy? How would they vote in referenda involving the issue? Would they vote to accept a clergywoman as minister for their congregation? Would they discriminate against clergywomen on the basis of sex?

The questionnaire included several items designed to measure differences in this aspect of receptivity to women in ministry. The first of these involved the simple matter of willingness to <u>accept</u> women clergy. Members of the free churches were asked the following question:

"If a qualified woman were ever recommended to the congregation, would you be willing to accept such a woman?

Fully <u>eighty-six percent</u> of the members in the free churches answered, "yes," they would accept a qualified woman as minister of their congregation.

In order to get at this idea among the Anglicans, since they have not yet endorsed the ordination of women denominationally, we asked a slightly different question. First we asked whether they had taken part in parish discussions of the ordination of women as priests. Contrary to the perception of some denominational spokespersons, only 15 per cent of the members indicated that they had actually participated in those debates. Of those 15 per cent who voted, 78 per cent stated that they had voted in <u>favor</u> of ordaining women as priests.

We also asked the Anglican members how they would vote on the ordination of women as priests if they were "voting on the issue today." About 61 per cent of them said they would vote in favor of the idea today. So we have an interesting contrast. Of the Anglican church members who had already participated in the discussions of the ordination of women, about 78 per cent stated that they had resolved the issue in favor of ordaining women. In the absence of any previous involvement in such discussions, however, significantly fewer members were willing to endorse the idea. This pattern implies that the more the issues are discussed openly, the more church members are likely to come down on the side of endorsing women's ordination. The concept of ordaining women as priests is very new to most lay church members. In the absence of some systematic exploration of the idea, it is easy for those who have not formulated an opinion to simply say they oppose it. With discussion, however, it appears that they tend to become more willing to explore the possibility of such change.

The next query of the Anglican respondents concerned how they would vote on two related issues. The first of these dealt with the ordination of women as deacons. Specifying that we were <u>not</u> referring to the position of "deaco<u>ness</u>," we asked the members how they would vote on that question. Seventy per cent indicated they would vote in favor of ordaining women as deacons. The second additional item concerned treatment of women already ordained as priests abroad, i.e. the following item:

"Some women have been ordained as priests in an Anglican Communion abroad (such as in Canada). Now and then one of them asks to be allowed to function as a priest in England. What do you think the answer to their request should be?"

Two-thirds of the members indicated that in their opinion women ordained abroad should be allowed to function as priests in England.

Combining these sets of responses from members of the free churches and the Anglican Church, it is possible to make a few generalizations. First, a majority of church members in all denominations indicated that they will accept women as ordained clergy. The proportions ranged from 93 per cent of Methodists to 61 per cent of

Anglicans. Second, therefore, it is apparent that there are denominational differences in this regard. Members of the free churches tend to be considerably more willing to accept ordained women clergy than are their Anglican counterparts. (We shall examine such denominational differences in receptivity in another stage of the analysis below.) Finally, as was the case in the members' preferences for men or women in clergy roles, overall at least three-fourths of the members are comfortable with the concept of women in pastoral roles. Most lay church members are well prepared to accept the implications of the sex role changes which accompany the influence of modern consciousness on religious organizations.

Willingness to discriminate:

Finally, we asked the members of the free churches a question which served to indicate their relative willingness to discriminate against female candidates for the pastorate of their congregation. The question was worded as follows:

"If tensions were to arise in the congregation because a woman had been recommended (as minister), which of the following actions do you think the (search committee) should take?

Stick with their recommendation and try to convince the church to call the woman. (35%)

Withdraw the woman's name and recommend a man instead. (8%)

Do nothing, but let the majority of the church decide what to do. (57%)

Those who asserted that the committee should stick with their recommendation were saying that they should not discriminate against the woman because of a threat of local controversy. By contrast, those who stated that the woman's name should be withdrawn were saying just the opposite, i.e. that the congregation should discriminate against the woman. These replies are clear. Members who said the committee should do nothing but let the majority of the congregation decide what to do were implying that the congregation should (or should not) discriminate depending on majority opinion.

It is noteworthy that only 8 per cent of the members were willing to discriminate against a woman outright. At the other extreme, slightly more than one-third said that the committee should "stick to their guns." It is the 57 per cent who said the committee should defer to majority rule that is potentially troublesome. On the one hand, it is likely that this pattern represents long-standing decision-making practices within free-church congregations. Most matters of congregational concern are decided by majority vote. On the other hand, however, it is somewhat disquieting to note that nearly two-thirds of the members were willing to discriminate against clergywomen at least in the name of majority rule. Here we have a conflict of principles. By deferring to the tradition of democratic decision-making practices, the members are upholding hard-won principles of congregational autonomy. But in the process of making the decision on the fate of the female candidate in this manner, the values of equality and justice are placed in considerable jeopardy. The underlying difference in this instance is the concern about dissensus and conflict in the congregation. This factor appears to be an important one in the women-in-ministry discussions, and we shall look at it systematically in a later stage of the analysis.

SUMMARY

Skeletal though it is, at this point we have a basic description of some ways in which lay church members in England respond to secularization of sex roles in church leadership. The results of a national-sample survey of those members indicate that most of them were able to deal with the prospective changes quite well. They did not appear to be threatened by the advent of clergywomen, and they were satisfied that the church can adapt to the change successfully.

The members did differ in the extent to which they view women ministers in traditional stereotyped terms. But most of them manifested their own assimilation of modern consciousness by rejecting most such stereotypes and by conceiving of women ministers in open and flexible terms.

The members also indicated little desire to retain men in the church leadership roles men have traditionally held. Instead the majority of members stated that they would be satisfied with either a man or a woman performing most traditional clergy functions, although they did split evenly on their preferences for men in the position of solo pastor or priest. Finally, less than one member in ten in the free churches was willing to discriminate outright against a woman candidate for the pastorate of a local congregation.

From these data it seems clear that most church members in these denominations in England are comfortable with modern consciousness as it manifests itself in pressures for changes in church leadership. The prospect of ordaining women -- a very recent innovation in church history -- is something they can live with. They appear satisfied that they can adapt to this departure from tradition and that the church will be none the worse for it.

In the next few chapters, we shall shift away from this descriptive mode of analysis toward a search for explanations. In the most general sense, we shall try to answer the question of why church members differ in their acceptance of women clergy. The discussion will focus especially on several ways in which the internalization of modern consciousness accounts for differences in members' openness to women in ministry.

CHAPTER 3
EXPLAINING PATTERNS OF RESISTANCE
MEMBER TRAITS

The patterns shown in Chapter 2 support a number of descriptive generalizations. The broadest of these points is that British church members differ widely in the extent to which they have developed a modern consciousness which they apply to sex roles in the churches. Some members view the possibility of having women as ordained clergy in very traditional terms and thus also tend to oppose this sort of change in church leadership. Others view the emergence of women in ministry in a less sacred mode, and they tend to be more approving of the innovation.

These differences showed up in survey data involving measures of three dimensions of attitudes towards women clergy -- varying perceptions of what clergywomen are like, differences in preferences for men or women in clergy roles, and readiness to accept or reject female candidates for the position of minister of a congregation. Among Anglicans there were also variations in willingness to endorse the ordination of women abroad and in acceptance of the idea of women as ordained deacons.

EXPLAINING DIFFERENCES IN RECEPTIVITY

With an image of these three facets of receptivity in mind, we now shift to the second major purpose of the study, i.e. explaining differences in attitude. Why do some people stereotype more than others? Why do some members prefer males in a variety of clergy roles, while others have no such preferences? Why are some members prepared to discriminate against women candidates and others not? In general, how can we account for these variations in acceptance of women as clergy?

To ask for an explanation is to ask for a theory. The bulk of the remainder of the analysis consists of a search for evidence that some theories about sex-role attitudes are applicable to differences in receptivity to women in ministry. Much of that analysis involves a series of comparisons of these differences in resistance to clergywomen with other attributes of church members. Where particular characteristics of members tend to be systematically associated with differences in receptivity, those relationships may shed light on the question of why such divergent attitudes exist.

Demographic Characteristics and Modern Consciousness

Consistent with the theoretical stance articulated in Chapter 1, we first look again at the concept of modern consciousness. If attitudes toward sex roles in the churches are manifestations of a modern, secularized form of consciousness, then members manifesting personal characteristics associated with that world view should manifest less religious sexism than those whose outlooks are more traditional.

1. Age

One factor which has been identified in other research as consistently predictive of variations in sex-role attitudes is age (e.g., Carroll, et al, 1983; and Lehman, 1985). Older persons tend to be more conservative than young people on sex-role issues. This pattern makes sense from the perspective of modern consciousness for at least two reasons. First, the older people were socialized in another age, usually one that contained cultural patterns which the present period is leaving behind, ways of thinking and acting once considered "natural" but now being questioned. Younger persons, on the other hand, never participated in those folkways, and they see no reason to place much importance on them.

Second, older persons sometimes have a vested interest in traditional social and cultural forms. For example, they may have spent their working life in an occupation which is threatened with obsolescence, thus seeming to demean the significance of their very life. They may have participated in family patterns which no longer enjoy a monopoly in the community, and as they see new forms proliferating, they sense the judgement of history that their old customs were not very important. By contrast, many younger people do not sense that they have much stake in past practices, and they tend to be quite prepared to innovate with limited regard for the consequences. No doubt at times this readiness to discard the past also bespeaks a sophomoric recklessness, but that problem is not at issue here. The point, rather, is simply that it is not hard to understand why younger people may be more in tune with modern consciousness than are their elders. If this is the case, then we should also see more young members than older ones prepared to accept women in ministry.

Table 3.1 shows correlations between differences in resistance to clergywomen and several demographic variables. Some correlations involving "age" shown in the table tend to support the above assertion, but not without exception. Older members tend to stereotype clergywomen more than do younger members, especially in terms of the "general reliability" aspect of that dimension. More older members than younger ones perceive women clergy as generally unreliable church workers. The relationship between age and "role-conflict" stereotyping is in the same direction -- more old than young members view clergywomen as unable to handle the cross pressures of job and home. However, the correlation is considerably weaker than that involving the "reliability" dimension. I would speculate that this difference is due to some older persons having had personal experiences which belie the stereotype and which, therefore, lead some of them to reject it.

2. Social Class

A second variable associated with modern consciousness is social class, especially the criteria which define class in modern industrial societies, i.e. occupation, education, and income. Persons engaged in high status occupations, first of all, are the more likely to develop world views associated with modern consciousness, because of their training and the social worlds in which they move. As to training, persons in professions, corporate management, and technical jobs learn to make rational decisions based on rational and technical criteria. In many instances, provincial folkways have no place in them. For the physician, for example, accurate diagnosis and appropriate treatment are primary values. Under those guidelines, technical and organizational innovations will be welcomed to the extent that they facilitate progress toward those goals. Similarly, managers of large commercial and industrial enterprises are trained to develop and implement corporate policies which maximize efficiency and profit while minimizing waste and other costs. These constellations of cultural patterns are the essence of modern consciousness, and they illustrate its pragmatic flexibility and its desire to be free from traditional constraints.

TABLE 3.1 CORRELATIONS (GAMMA) BETWEEN MEASURES OF RECEPTIVITY/RESISTANCE TO WOMEN IN MINISTRY AND SELECTED DEMOGRAPHIC CHARACTERISTICS OF PROTESTANT LAY CHURCH MEMBERS IN ENGLAND

	age	sex	occup'n	educ'n	income	community size	region
reliability stereotyping score	.23	ns*	.11	.15	.24	.07	ns
role conflict stereotyping score	.08	ns	ns	ns	.08	ns	ns
sacramental gender preference score	.08	ns	ns	.07	.11	ns	ns
organizational gender preference score	.20	ns	.10	.14	.21	ns	ns
will accept qualified woman	ns	ns	ns	ns	ns	ns	Midlands/"yes"
FREE CHURCHES ONLY:							
willingness to discriminate	ns	ns	ns	ns	ns	.09	ns
ANGLICANS ONLY:							
reject women as deacons	ns	ns	ns	ns	.23	ns	ns
reject women ordained abroad	.16	ns	.15	ns	.31	.15	ns

* indicates a statistically nonsignificant correlation.

Second, persons who work in such occupations also tend to have more varied culture contacts than those who work in more routinized pursuits. These contacts are likely to erode some allegiances to tradition and enhance the development of new perspectives on social and cultural life in general. These differences should also involve more liberal attitudes towards sex roles.

The figures contained in Table 3.1 indicate that such differences in occupation are associated with some dimensions of receptivity but not others. Where there is a significant correlation, the relationship is in the direction one would expect. Being in a high-status occupation tends to be associated with a liberal stance towards women in ministry, and working in pursuits with less prestige, power, and autonomy is more often linked to conservative attitudes. Persons in high-status areas of work tend to stereotype women ministers less than those in low-status fields in terms of perceptions of women's general reliability. They also have fewer preferences for men in organizational clergy roles. Among the Anglicans, more members in high-status occupations than low-status fields approved of allowing women ordained abroad to function as priests in England.

Formal education is associated with the development of modern consciousness in a similar fashion. As persons develop skills in critical thinking, problem solving, quantitative analysis, verbal facility, etc., and as they internalize the substance of various intellectual pursuits -- history, philosophy, science, etc. they realize the complexity of various levels of reality and how little we actually know about them. They also tend to reject various simplistic aspects of the folk culture, recognizing them as inadequate. These aspects of personal and intellectual growth are antithetical to most provincial modes of relating to social and cultural issues. As people develop such perspectives, therefore, they tend to be more open than less well educated persons to innovations of many kinds.

There is some evidence in the figures in Table 3.1 to support the notion that formal education is related in these ways to attitudes towards women in ministry. Where the analysis resulted in statistically significant correlations between formal education and various dimensions of receptivity to clergywomen, the associations were in the predicted direction. Education was positively related to receptivity to women in ministry. More members with high levels of education than with little formal training manifested open and flexible perceptions of clergywomen in terms of their general reliability. Education was also positively related to acceptance of women in both sacramental and organizational clergy roles. The more educated the member, the more likely he/she was to view women as capable of performing liturgical functions well and of managing the organizational machinery of the church for the good of the congregation.

The results were even more consistent concerning the family income of the members. (See Table 3.1.) On every dimension of receptivity but one, i.e. willingness to discriminate, the more income the members made, the more favorable they were to the advent of women in ministry.

Accordingly, these patterns offer some further support for the proposition that differences in attitudes towards women clergy are partly a result of modern consciousness. <u>Members with educational, economic, and social resources associated with that orientation tended to manifest less religious sexism than those not possessing such characteristics.</u>

3. Sex

Among casual observers, sex is typically expected to play a major role in determining receptivity to women in ministry. Feminists argue that it is the men who are the more resistant to clergywomen, because the movement of women into clergy ranks erodes a male power base and places men at risk of being subordinate to women. Some men, on the other hand, especially some denominational administrators, are convinced that it is the female church members who are the more opposed to women in ministry. Their argument often involves laywomen's supposed resentment over not having a minister's wife to be involved in various "ladies'" functions and over not having the male figure in the pulpit about whom they can fantasize in various ways. Such arguments predict opposite outcomes.

Some previous work in the United States supports the idea that it is the men who are the more resistant to the ordination of women (e.g. Carroll, et al, 1983; and Lehman, 1985). However, these relationships have not been very strong. And in one other study, there was no association between sex and acceptance of clergywomen (Lehman, 1979).

The results shown in Table 3.1 indicate that sex is also not a good predictor of resistance to women in ministry in England. There was no significant correlation between sex and any dimension of receptivity. The entry of women into the ordained ministry is neither exclusively a "male problem" nor a "female problem." It is neither, and it is both.

4. Community Type

The final type of variable compared with resistance to clergywomen in this section was community type. We approached this factor in two ways: community size and region.

The analysis included the variable "community size" to get at the rural-urban dichotomy which has sometimes proven useful in other work. We measured this factor by asking the ministers and parish priests to characterize the community of their congregation in terms of whether it was:

1. a large city (over 100,000) - 23%
2. a small city (25,000-99,999) - 19%
3. a small town (2,500-24,999) - 30%
4. a village or rural area (under 2,500) - 28%.

The percentage distribution indicates that we obtained a varied sample in this regard.

One might expect urban living to be associated with a greater number of culture contacts than is rural life. City dwellers may also experience more rational economic orientations than do rural people. If this is the case, then one might expect urban dwellers to manifest more signs of modern consciousness than rural folk. We correlated community size with the indicators of religious sexism, and the results are also shown in Table 3.1. The figures show that on most dimensions of resistance, there were no significant differences by size of place. The three dimensions which did turn out to be related to community size -- reliability stereotyping, willingness to discriminate, and Anglicans' acceptance of women ordained abroad -- were related as one would predict, but the correlations were weak. More members from small communities than large ones manifested religious sexism in terms of viewing women as unreliable church leaders, being prepared to discriminate against female candidates, and (for Anglicans) rejecting women ordained abroad.

The variable "region" was even less useful. Only one coefficient was statistically significant. Members living in the Midlands were slightly more prepared finally to "accept" a qualified woman minister than were those from the other two regions. One might speculate that the equal-employment motif typically associated with secular industry might have something to do with this result -- the Midlands is more heavily industrialized than other sections of the country. This ethos could make those living there more sensitive to the issue than those living elsewhere. But if this were the case, one would also expect similar results on their willingness to discriminate against female candidates. This result was not forthcoming. The safest conclusion at this point is that regional differences are not very predictive of variations in religious sexism.

Summary

To this point the analysis has given some support to the theory that the extent to which church members have developed modern consciousness influences their resistance and receptivity to women in ministry -- their religious sexism. This is especially the case involving age and social class. The theory would lead us to expect to observe the effects of modern consciousness more among the young than the old, and more among higher social strata than lower. Where indicators of these variables were significantly correlated, the relationship was in the direction predicted. There were no correlations in the opposite direction as to contradict the theory.

However, at least two caveats are necessary at this point. First, the effects of these variables appear to be mainly on tendencies to stereotype and gender preferences for clergy roles, effects which occur early in the path of effects on eventual acceptance of women in ministry (see Lehman, 1981a). These variables have little if any direct effect on willingness to discriminate against clergywomen or on eventual acceptance of a qualified woman in the role of minister. Yet they were predictive of some facets of the issue unique to the Anglican community.

Second, type of community -- a variable some would expect to be associated with the development of modern consciousness -- was only minimally related to the prevalence of sexism. Community size was predictive of sexism as one would predict from the theory, but only on a few dimensions. And regional differences were virtually non-existent. Social reality is more complex than the theory can encompass.

Religious Involvement and Modern Consciousness

Modern consciousness has been characterized as "secularized" consciousness. That is, it involves a readiness to question traditional social and cultural patterns and to entertain alternative modes of structuring subjective and objective reality (Berger, 1969). As such it is sometimes antithetical to uncritical involvement in routinized modes of community life. This principle can be applied to all areas of possible participation -- politics, family, leisure, etc. It can also illumine patterns of traditional religious involvements. The more individuals develop an open stance towards various modern modes of relating to the world, the less likely they are to find traditional (especially "folk") patterns of religious thought and action immediately satisfying. Again, this is not to say that such persons are no longer "religious." Rather the concept asserts that they are less likely to be content with traditional forms of religious life.

If this is the case, then we should also find degrees of traditional religious involvement positively related to religious sexism. The more church members manifest traditional modes of involvement in religious life, the more likely they should be to resist women as ordained clergy.

Some previous work on these relationships in the United States supports that argument (e.g. Lehman, 1979; 1985). The general pattern has been that the more traditionally involved in religious systems the member is, the more likely that person is to be opposed to women in ministry. Is this also the case among British church members?

The results of comparing measures of religious sexism to indicators of religious involvement are contained in Table 3.2. The first two columns deal with differences in overt involvement in religious life -- attendance at public worship services and engaging in private prayer at meals ("saying grace"). The measures of these variable were quite straightforward. The measure of pietistic private prayer was:

"About how often do you say grace at meals?
 daily -- 22%
 weekly -- 8%
 on special occasions -- 45%
 never" -- 26%

The results in the table indicate that frequency of saying grace at meals was predictive of the extent to which church members stereotype women in ministry,

TABLE 3.2 CORRELATIONS (GAMMA) BETWEEN MEASURES OF RECEPTIVITY/RESISTANCE TO WOMEN IN MINISTRY AND SELECTED RELIGIOUS CHARACTERISTICS OF PROTESTANT LAY CHURCH MEMBERS IN ENGLAND

	church attendance	saying grace	value on evangelism	value on reform	importance of reunion with Rome#
reliability stereotyping score	ns**	.14	.08	-.10	ns
role conflict stereotyping score	.11	.16	.11	-.13	ns
sacramental gender preference score	ns	.11	.11	-.14	.15
organizational gender preference score	ns	.13	.08	-.10	ns
will accept qualified woman	ns	-.21	-.17	.23	-.17
FREE CHURCHES ONLY:					
willingness to discriminate	ns	.19	.13	-.16	----
ANGLICANS ONLY:					
reject women as deacons	ns	ns	.22	-.12	.16
reject women ordained abroad	.21	ns	.29	-.27	ns

** indicates a statistically non-significant correlation.

an issue considered among Anglicans only.

preferred men in clergy roles, would accept a qualified woman as pastor, and were prepared to discriminate against female candidates for their congregation's minister. Involvement in traditional pietistic ritual was associated with resistance to women clergy. However, variations in frequency of private ritual prayer were not related to the Anglicans' attitudes toward women as deacons and the functioning of women ordained abroad. Nevertheless, with this last exception, the results are consistent with the theory; traditional religious involvement is associated with several aspects of religious sexism.

Involvement in public ritual, however, did not appear to be predictive of most dimensions of attitudes towards clergywomen. The question measuring differences in public ritual involvement was:

"About how often do you attend worship services? Would it be:

nearly every week -- 86%

once or twice a month -- 9%

several times a year -- 4%

rarely or never" -- 1%

The more members attended Sunday worship services, the more they engaged in role-conflict stereotyping and, among the Anglicans, the more they rejected women ordained abroad. On the other dimensions of receptivity, however, church attendance was not predictive of attitudinal differences. These results may indicate that differences in traditional public ritual involvements have little to do with attitudes towards women in ministry. However, the outcome is more likely an artifact of the questionnaire item used to measure church attendance. In spite of numerous cautions taken in the design of the data-collection instrument, the response categories listed for this item proved to be inappropriate. The eventual

responses were highly skewed -- 86 per cent in the highest
category ("nearly every week") -- so the item did not
discriminate adequately at this end of the continuum.
Given findings in other studies in the United States,
where church attendance has been consistently associated
with resistance to clergywomen (e.g. Lehman, 1979: 1985),
the divergent outcome appears more likely to be an
artifact of this failure in operationalization.

The third aspect of religious commitment we
considered was religious ideology, cognitive orientation
rather than overt action. We approached this concept by
focusing on one facet of the members' ecclesiology, their
concept of the church. In an effort to determine what the
members considered important in congregational life -- and
thus probably in Christian life in general -- we asked
them the following question:

"People often differ regarding the relative
importance of various aspects of congregational life.
Four such aspects are listed below.

Please indicate which aspect is most important to you
by writing the number "1" beside it. Then write the
number "2" by the next most important, the number "3"
by the third, and the number "4" by the fourth in
importance. PLEASE DO NOT USE A NUMBER MORE THAN
ONCE.

rank   aspect

1   worshipping God as part of a community of people
       seeking to follow Christ

2   seeking to help individuals who cannot help
       themselves

3   trying to convert people to faith in Christ

4   trying to solve social problems outside the
       church through social reform."

(The aspects were listed in a different order on the

questionnaire.) The overall ranking of these items among the members of all four denominations (viewed both separately and as a whole) was in the order listed above. The worshipping community was typically listed first, and work to solve social problems was usually listed last.

The ranking of two of these items proved to be predictive of differences in receptivity to women in ministry, one traditional -- the evangelism function-- and the other quite non-traditional -- the social reform emphasis. As shown in Table 3.2, the more value members placed on evangelism, the more they were opposed to clergywomen on all dimensions of resistance. Conversely, the more value they placed on church involvement in social reform activities, the more receptive they were to the idea of clergywomen. The more traditional function was associated with resistance to women in ministry, whereas the more non-traditional function was associated with acceptance. This is what one would expect to observe based on a theory of the effects of modern consciousness.

The final column in Table 3.2 indicates the results of using a question asked only of the Anglican church members:

"The Church of England is engaged in discussions with the Roman Catholic Church about possible reunification of the two bodies into one church. How important is this issue to you personally? Would it be:

very important -- 54%
slightly important -- 22%
not very important -- 16%
not important at all" -- 8%

The pattern of responses to the question indicates that overall the issue tends to be considered important. More than three-fourths of the Anglican church members indicated that the matter had at least some importance to them personally.

We included this item in the questionnaire, because in informal conversations some observers had suggested that the ordination of women as clergy would impede progress towards reunification with Rome. The more people were concerned about this, it was argued, the more likely they were to oppose women in ministry. Was this in fact the case?

The correlations in Table 3.2 suggest a partial confirmation of the prediction. The importance of the reunion issue was related to gender preferences in sacramental roles, final acceptance of a qualified woman, and acceptance of women as deacons. The more members stressed the issue, the more conservative they were on these aspects of sexism. However, the importance of reunification with Rome was not related to members' perceptions of what clergywomen are like. This pattern makes sense. A member primarily concerned about the impact of women's ordination on cooperation with other denominations (rather than on ordination itself) is likely to prefer males for priests and not be prepared to accept women as clergy. But the problem would not necessarily affect such persons' perceptions of what women ministers are like.

SUMMARY

In this chapter we began to address the question of how to explain variations in the prevalence of sexism among church members. The theory examined was the perspective on which the discussion has focused from the outset -- the development of modern consciousness. If that mode of relating to the world is as described, then

church members who are characterized by modern
consciousness should manifest less religious sexism than
those whose outlooks are more traditional.

The analysis to this point gives some support to the
theory that receptivity/resistance to women in ministry is
related to individual differences in the development of
modern forms of consciousness. The more individual church
members manifested characteristics associated with modern
consciousness, the less they also showed indications of
religious sexism -- resistance to women in ministry.
This pattern was apparent in comparisons of the indicators
of sexism with measures of age, education, occupation, and
income. There was also marginal support in correlations
involving community size. There were no correlations in
the direction that would serve to falsify the theory.

The relationships between indicators of resistance to
women clergy and traditional religious involvement also
tend to support the idea that differences in religious
sexism may be understood in terms of the development of
modern consciousness. The more the members were
personally involved in traditional ritual and ideological
patterns of religious participation, a pattern usually
antithetical to modern consciousness, the more they tended
to oppose women in ministry on one dimension or another.

In the next chapter, we continue the consideration of
modern consciousness as a factor in religious sexism by
examining a variable closely related to that type of world
outlook, i.e. the local/cosmopolitan dichotomy.

CHAPTER 4
LOCALISM AND SEXISM

In the preceding discussion, we examined evidence from the survey of British church members linking religious sexism to a series of correlates of modern consciousness. The general tendency was for persons possessing characteristics associated with the development of modern consciousness to be less sexist than those whose world outlooks were more traditional. Attributes which were related to differences in world outlook this way involved some familiar demographic factors and modes of traditional religious involvement.

This chapter deals with the possible relationships between modern consciousness and religious sexism in terms of the "local/cosmopolitan" dichotomy, a perspective which has enjoyed renewed popularity during the last decade, particularly in the work of Roof (1974; 1976; 1978). Roof's goal was to use the local/cosmopolitan dichotomy to explain the widely perceived relationship between conservative religiosity and several types of prejudice and other social conservatism. He summarizes the work by saying, "localistic orientations are associated with conservative religious beliefs and traditional minority prejudices." "If localistic world views are conceptualized as reified social perspectives, it is not surprising that orthodox beliefs and minority attitudes covary together." "The observed association between religious orthodoxy and prejudice...may be largely spurious..." and instead may be due to some effects of localism (1974:660). The patterns of relationships Roof conceptualized are illustrated in the path model shown in Figure 4.1 (Roof, 1978:48), where prejudice is portrayed as an artifact of local community identification.

Figure 4.1

CONCEPTUAL MODEL FOR A LOCAL-COSMOPOLITAN THEORY
OF CONSERVATIVE RELIGIOSITY AND ITS CONSEQUENCES

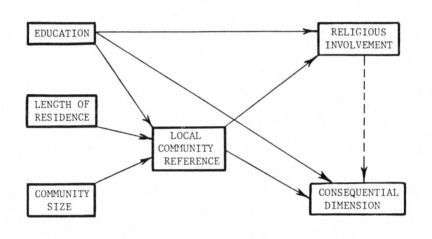

———————————— basic causal relations

— — — — — — weak, questionable relations

The local/cosmopolitan dichotomy may be useful in the present discussion, because it involves conceptual space which is close to the construct of modern consciousness. As demonstrated below, the two conceptualizations are similar in that they refer to parallel ways in which persons relate to the world around them. They involve contrasts between a narrow, tradition-bound, and largely uninformed provincialism on the one hand, in contrast to a broad, secularized, and informed universalism on the other.

If minority prejudice and religious involvement are partly epiphenomenal of localistic orientations, then it is possible that the same logic applies to sexism. We have already indicated how the idea of modern consciousness fits into the picture. Before incorporating the local/cosmopolitan variable into the analysis, let us review briefly the logic of that concept and see how it may be related to religious sexism.

The Local/Cosmopolitan Dichotomy

Roof defined the distinctions between locals and cosmopolitans in terms similar to those of Merton (1957): i.e. "their patterns of social participation, and their orientations to the world around them..., social belonging and...world view and meaning" (Roof, 1978:42). "Locals are more attached to their immediate social locale and are quite sensitive to the primary groups in which they interact, such as the family, neighborhood cliques, and community organizations." "Cosmopolitans have their commitments centered outside the residential community and tend to identify more with abstract, generalized groups that may be spatially remote, such as their profession or the corporation in which they work" (1978:41).

The local-cosmopolitan distinction has cropped up in discussions of a variety of issues -- social influence (Merton, 1957), organizational behavior (Gouldner, 1957-58), lifestyle (Dobriner, 1958), political ideology (Dye, 1963; Ladd, 1972), community participation (Lehman, 1964), prejudice (Liu, 1960; Roof, 1974), and social activism (Ammerman, 1981). Locals tend to be traditional and conservative, while cosmopolitans are inclined towards progressivism and liberalism. The analysis below seeks to determine whether these patterns also apply in the case of sexism in religious institutions, i.e. attitudes towards women in ministry.

Dimensions of Localism

An examination of research involving localism suggests that the concept may be broken down into different types or dimensions, different ways in which people may be classified as "local" or "cosmopolitan." Two such dimensions are reflected in some indicators used in previous work. They correspond to two recurrent themes in localism research, i.e. "world view" and "social belonging." Roof's (1974; 1976; 1978) work, first of all, involves measures which appear to tap a "cultural" aspect of localism (see also Dobriner, 1958; and Dye, 1963):

1. "Despite all the newspaper and TV coverage, national and international happenings rarely seem as interesting as events that occur in the local community in which one lives."

2. "Big cities may have their place, but the local community is the backbone of America."

3. "When it comes to choosing someone for a responsible public office in my community, I prefer a person whose family is known and well established locally."

4. "The most rewarding organizations a person can belong to are the large, state- and nation-wide associations rather than local community clubs and activities."

With the possible exception of the fourth item, these indicators concentrate on a "cultural" dimension of localism, the assertion that "local is better than extra-local." This facet of localism deals with the values and meanings associated with local and extra-local symbols, events, and issues, i.e. aspects of "culture." The culturally local person would feel that locality-oriented life styles are of intrinsic and primary importance. He/she would assume that "local" is good, noble, valuable, and important, while extra-local entities and events are of secondary or tertiary importance. Cosmopolitans would feel otherwise.

Roof's items also tend to embody a concept of localism which is not community-specific, i.e. they tend to refer to "local things in general." Instead of dealing with the person's particular community, items #1, #2, and #4 ask about local communities generically -- "local-ness" in the abstract, instead of "my" or "your" specific community -- any local community, not a particular locale.

This cultural flavor of Roof's measures is very different from the content of the measures employed by Kasarda and Janowitz (1974:331) in their study of localism in Great Britain. The items used in their research reflect more of a "social" and particularistic localism. They are as follows:

1. "Is there an area around here where you are now living which you would say you belong to, where you feel 'at home'?"

2. "How interested are you to know what goes on in (home area)?"

3. "Supposing that for some reason you had to move away from (home area), how sorry or pleased would you be to leave?"

These items focus not on locality in general or on the abstract meaning or value of the local community, but on concrete and specific communities. "Do you feel at home here?" "Are you interested in what goes on in this place?" "Would you be sorry to have to move from here?"

These indicators reflect a "social" dimension of localism. They deal with the extent to which individuals identify with their locale and their structural relations there. They reflect the issue of social involvement in specific sets of relationships.

Each of these sets of items has been employed in empirical investigations of the local/cosmopolitan dichotomy. At first glance they all appear to have sufficient face validity to justify their use as measures of the localism concept. But closer examination suggests that the two approaches are not merely different ways of measuring the same construct. Instead they are measures of conceptually important and different dimensions of localism -- one cultural and the other social-structural. Cultural localism embodies what some individuals have labelled the "myopia" of small-town life. Social localism, on the other hand, is more comparable to reference group theory. The cultural dimension deals with the values and meanings involved in local community life in general, while the social facet concentrates on the importance of relationships with specific people in a particular place.

Cultural Localism and Modern Consciousness

It is the "cultural" aspect of the local/cosmopolitan concept which is of interest for this analysis, i.e. "world view" or "meaning." The distinction between cultural localism and cosmopolitanism, especially as operationalized by Roof (see above), involves a variable closely related to the contrast between traditional and modern consciousness. Work on localism characterizes locals as narrow, provincial, concrete in thought patterns, intolerant, and socially conservative. Discussions of modern consciousness characterize persons who have not developed that Weltanschauung as tradition-bound, reifying in thought patterns, ethnocentric, temperocentric and slow to accept social and cultural change. It is highly likely that valid indicators of the two variables would be intercorrelated. They are getting at similar perspectives.

This is not to say that localism can be reduced to traditional consciousness or that traditional consciousness is but localism writ large. The concept of "localism" has an intrinsic locality frame of reference, while the construct "modes of consciousness" makes no such geographic stipulations. The point instead is that there is conceptual overlap in the orientational aspects of the two concepts. Persons categorized as "cultural locals" are likely to manifest world perspectives which modernity theorists would classify as "traditional consciousness," and persons described in secularization theory as having developed "little modern consciousness" are also likely to be classified by localism theorists as "locals."

Accordingly, an examination of relationships between cultural localism and religious sexism should be helpful in our attempts to explain variations in the latter. In fact, indicators of cultural localism are likely to serve as more direct measures of styles of consciousness than were the correlates involved in the preceding chapter. The analysis below proceeds on that assumption.

Ecclesiological Localism

A second dimension of localism incorporated in this analysis is "ecclesiological localism," another form of difference in orientation which is related to the idea of modern consciousness in much the same way as cultural localism. "Ecclesiological localism" refers to church members' understanding of what "church" means. Some individuals conceptualize "church" in highly local terms, i.e. as a congregation in a specific locale, a building in a particular place with its own cemetery and unique approaches to worship, funerals, weddings, and other aspects of day-to-day church life. "Church" to them is a concrete entity one can point to in physical terms. It has a name which separates it from another congregation and building in the next town or a few blocks down the road. This is "ecclesiological localism."

For others the concept of "church" is not so geographically focused. These individuals conceive of the church as a more diffuse community. Instead of being identified with a local congregation in a specific building, "church" for these others is coterminous with a body of co-religionists encompassing at least the larger society (or nation) if not the entire Christian community in all parts of the globe. Church, for them, is not only "here" but also "out there." They also view "church" in less temperocentric terms. They are likely to view it as part of a historical community stretching back into early Judaeo-Christian times and forward to future generations of believers or communicants. These people are "ecclesiological cosmopolitans."

The description of ecclesiological localism above is couched in terms analogous to cultural localism -- assumptions about "the" church -- any church. One can also conceive of ecclesiological localism in a mode comparable to social localism as well -- i.e. attachments to particular congregations, to "this" church -- but this analysis will deal only with the former dimension.

In the analysis below, we shall correlate measures of cultural localism and ecclesiological localism with measures of receptivity to women in ministry. The question we will seek to answer is whether these forms of localism, concepts whose logic overlaps the modern consciousness argument, are predictive of variations in religious sexism in the form of resistance to women as ordained clergy. If the conceptual overlap is real, we should find both cultural and ecclesiological locals manifesting more religious sexism than cultural and ecclesiological cosmopolitans.

Indicators

The items used to measure differences in each dimension of localism are contained in Table 4.1. The questions listed under "cultural localism" are the items used by Roof with minor changes in spelling and terminology to adapt them to the British scene. The ecclesiological localism items were constructed from scratch for use in this investigation. As indicators of the respondents' orientations towards "church" as local or cosmopolitan, the items possess sufficient face validity as to render them useful. (On the data collection instrument itself, all localism items were placed in a random sequence so as to avoid obtaining a response set.)

A few patterns are apparent from an examination of the responses to the localism items. First, it is clear that the overall tendency among the church members is to appear predominantly local in orientation. More members appear to be localistic both in general cultural terms and in terms of their concept of "church." Only one cultural localism item suggests an even division between locals and cosmopolitans, and that is the fourth one on the list. Similarly, two out of three ecclesiological localism items indicated a basically local orientation. The one showing greater prevalence of cosmopolitan tendencies is the question dealing with contributing money for programs beyond the local community. Nevertheless, the overall tendency is clearly for church members to manifest more

Table 4.1 PATTERNS OF RESPONSE TO MEASURES OF TWO TYPES OF LOCAL/COSMOPOLITANISM AMONG PROTESTANT LAY CHURCH MEMBERS IN ENGLAND

	strongly agree	agree slightly	disagree slightly	strongly disagree
CULTURAL LOCALISM				
Big cities may have their place, but it is the local community that is the back-bone of England.	65**	24	9	3
When it comes to choosing someone for a responsible public office in my community, I prefer a person whose family is known and well-established locally.	45	30	16	9
* The most rewarding organisations a person can belong to are the large, nationwide associations rather than local community clubs and activities.	6	13	37	44
Despite all the newspaper and TV coverage, national and international events rarely seem as interesting as events that occur in the local community where I live.	17	27	28	27

Table 4.1 (cont'd)

ECCLESIOLOGICAL LOCALISM

The truly important work of the church is accomplished more in the local congregation than in wider prlgrammes dealing with world problems.	43	33	17	7
* Local churches should be willing to make great sacrifices in order to be able to contribute money for programmes beyond the local community.	27	43	22	7
When it comes to a choice between the needs of the local church and of wider commitments of the Baptist Union, we must give priority to the local church.	47	32	15	6

* disagreement with this item indicates the "local" orientation, whereas agreement with the other items indicates localism.

** figures are in per cent

local tendencies than cosmopolitan ones. This pattern is consistent with impressionistic observations suggesting that church members as a group tend to be more localistic than cosmopolitan.

In spite of this tendency, however, there is sufficient variation in the responses to the total set of questions to indicate that the items did indeed tap a "variable" and do reflect useful measures of the concepts involved. Some members turn out to be "locals," while others appear to be "cosmopolitans."

Composite Indexes

For the sake of parsimony, in comparing these differences to measures of sexist attitudes and other variables, we combined each subset of localism items into a composite index for use in the analysis to follow. This procedure enabled us to assign each respondent a "cultural localism score" and an "ecclesiological localism score." The scoring was done by standardizing the coding within each subset and then simply summing the coded responses to each item in that subset.

There was one exception to this procedure involving the cultural localism items. The item dealing with "the most rewarding organizations" was excluded from the cultural localism index. We deleted this question because (1) it did not load with the other items in a factor analysis' and (2) it was not correlated in the same way as the other items in the analysis below. It is interesting to note in this regard that Peterson and Takayama (1983:308; and 1984:103) observed a similar pattern in their efforts to replicate Roof's work. The item on "rewarding organizations" did not load with the other cultural localism items in their factor analysis either.

These observations further reinforce the perception that this item is qualitatively different from the other three, i.e. it deals less exclusively with "cultural" localistic concerns, involving some aspects of the "social" identification dimension as well. Accordingly, there are both conceptual and empirical grounds for not including that item in the cultural localism index.

After generating the localism scores, we collapsed them around the median for the sake of manageability. The distributions of the two sets of scores are shown in Table 4.2. The distributions have roughly equal numbers of cases around the median, so any comparisons with other variables will involve sufficient numbers as to generate reliable statistics. Remember, however, that the median for each set of scores was skewed with the median tending to fall toward the "localism" end of the continuum.

Table 4.2

DISTRIBUTIONS (PERCENT) OF SCORES ON INDEXES
OF CULTURAL AND ECCLESIOLOGICAL LOCALISM

CULTURAL LOCALISM:

	Cosmopolitan		Local
score	1	2	3
percent	24	49	27

ECCLESIOLOGICAL LOCALISM:

	Cosmopolitan		Local
score	1	2	3
percent	24	49	27

RESULTS

If the results of earlier work relating localism to various forms of prejudice and conservatism are generalizable, then one would expect differences in localism to be associated with variations in sexism. Specifically, one would hypothesize that localism scores will be significantly correlated to the measures of religious sexism, with high localism associated with high sexism. The correlations between variables in the conceptual model are contained in Table 4.3. The coefficients indicate that most of the expected outcomes found empirical support, but a few others did not.

Table 4.3

RANK-ORDER CORRELATIONS BETWEEN MEASURES OF RESISTANCE
TO WOMEN IN MINISTRY AND TWO TYPES OF LOCALISM

	Cultural Localism Score	Ecclesiological Localism Score
Reliability Stereotyping Score	.34	.19
Role Conflict Stereotyping Score	.10	.07
Sacramental Preference Score	.21	.19
Organizational Preference Score	.28	.21
Will Accept Qualified Woman	-.13	-.15
Willingness to Discriminate	ns*	ns
Approve Women as Deacons**	ns	ns
Approve Women Ordained Abroad**	ns	ns

* a statistically non-significant correlation

** applies to Anglicans only

A number of patterns are apparent in the results. First, both cultural localism and ecclesiological localism tended to be predictive of resistance to women in ministry. High localism scores were associated with tendencies to stereotype clergywomen, to prefer men in clergy roles, and to be prepared to reject a qualified woman as minister of one's congregation.

However, the localism scores were not related to the facets of sexism associated with particular denominations. Willingness to discriminate against women candidates -- a factor applicable only to the Free Churches -- was not related to localism. And Anglicans' acceptance of women as deacons and of women ordained abroad were unrelated to localism.

Second, stereotyping scores and gender preference scores tended to be correlated more strongly with cultural localism than with ecclesiological localism. Differences in cultural localism were more predictive of members' perceptions of clergywomen and their preferences for men in clergy roles than were variations in ecclesiological localism. This difference is of interest because of its implications for the modern consciousness model. The indicators of cultural localism are more closely related to the concept of modern consciousness than are the items dealing with ecclesiological localism. The pattern lends further support, therefore, to the idea that variations in religious sexism can be explained in terms of the relative presence of modern consciousness.

Finally, the differences in the magnitude of the coefficients involving the two aspects of stereotyping are of some interest. Localism was more predictive of whether or not members viewed clergywomen as generally reliable than of whether they thought women clergy would be able to manage role conflict between job and home. The possible "reality check" many members have had concerning stereotypes about women handling role conflict apparently renders those perceptions less dependent on such factors as local or cosmopolitan world outlooks than is the case with reliability stereotyping.

SUMMARY

Given the possible conceptual overlap concerning the distinction between traditional and modern consciousness and the local/cosmopolitan dichotomy, we compared measures of two types of localism and resistance to women in ministry. One facet of localism was "cultural localism" as discussed and measured by Roof (1974; 1976; 1978), and the other was ecclesiological localism, defined in terms of the breadth with which one conceptualizes "the church." If the conceptual spaces involving modern consciousness and cosmopolitanism are as close as one would expect, and if Roof's discussions of localism and prejudice and social conservatism may be generalized to apply to sexism as well, then one should expect localism to be predictive of religious sexism.

The analysis tended to support such a prediction. Some of Roof's (1978) ideas and observations, especially the effects of localism as "breadth of perspective," apply to sexism in the same way as they do to other forms of prejudice and social conservatism. Cultural locals tend to be more sexist than do cosmopolitans.

The same pattern applies to ecclesiological localism. "Breadth of perspective" at the level of one's concept of the church is also predictive of sexism. Members who conceived of the church in very local terms tend to be more resistant to women in ministry than do those who view the church in more universalistic terms.

The analysis reported in the next chapter moves the discussion to a different level. Instead of examining variables at the individual level of analysis, such as "age," "social class," or "localism," the approach takes a look at aggregate factors -- denomination, the characteristics of the members' churches, etc. It expands our understanding of the scope of factors influencing church members' readiness to accept women as ordained clergy.

CHAPTER 5
SEXISM AND CHARACTERISTICS
OF DENOMINATIONS AND CONGREGATIONS

The analysis reported in chapters 3 and 4 presented evidence that several factors associated with modern consciousness were predictive of religious sexism among church members. Individuals with characteristics normally associated with modern consciousness -- in terms of age, social class, traditional religious involvement, etc.-- were less likely to manifest also resistance to women in ministry than were persons with the opposite sets of traits. Persons whose Weltanschauung inclined toward "localism," an orientation related to the rote of traditional consciousness, also tended to display more indications of sexism than did those whose orientations were more "cosmopolitan." Examination of these individual differences tended to support the argument that many variations in religious sexism can be explained in terms of the extent to which members have internalized a non-traditional cognitive style.

SOCIAL DETERMINANTS OF RELIGIOUS SEXISM

This chapter takes a different approach to the problem of explaining differences in receptivity to clergywomen. It deals with characteristics of groups and large organizations rather than of individuals. We move from the individual to the social level of analysis. Social factors can be at least as important as individual traits in explaining variations in social attitudes and actions.

At the heart of the sociological tradition is the general assumption that many differences in individual thought and action can be explained in terms of aggregate factors rather than individual traits. Shared characteristics of society, in the broadest sense culture and social organization, are major influences on social behavior. Individuals learn who they are and what they should and should not do from the community into which they are born or, for some, into which they move. Similarly, the structures of relationships between individuals, groups, and social strata constitute some of the mazes through which people try to figure out where they are going and how to get there.

One useful illustration of the importance of each level of analysis in human action is a symphony orchestra. In order for an orchestra to present what listeners would regard as a "good performance," sets of both individual and social characteristics must be present. (1) The individual performers must have the skill which the musical production requires, and (2) they must be sufficiently familiar with the particular composition (or at least their "part" in it) to apply those skills appropriately. Similarly, there has to be sufficient normative and structural organization for the group as a whole to act like "an orchestra." It requires much more than a mere aggregation of unique individuals. The characteristics of (3) the score must be such as to coordinate the efforts of individual musicians so that they can know when to execute specific techniques and other actions. There must also be (4) a proper balance (or at least nearly so) in the numbers of each type of musical instrument for the composer's intentions to be carried out. (5) The instrumentalists must be spatially arranged as to allow coordination and blend of their sound production. (6) There must be a working consensus about roles, authority, division of labor, and so forth.

None of these factors (and perhaps others as well) can be ignored with the confident expectation of producing sounds that listeners will consider a musical performance of a "symphony orchestra." The first two requirements listed above focus on characteristics of individuals, traits without which there will be no "adequate performance." The others are organizational factors, and they make critical differences too. Orchestras must be tightly organized and controlled. In accounting for "the performance," therefore, it is not productive to engage in either psychological or social reductionism. All levels of analysis yield insights which are useful for explaining what is going on.

The same principle applies to other kinds of social units, of course, to athletic teams, aircraft crews, factories -- and churches. All of them depend upon the existence of complex constellations of both individual and social factors for goal attainment and other outcomes of social action taking place within their arenas. And the various factors interact and influence each other. They do not function in isolation. Individual traits affect social characteristics, such as the conductor's wishes determining how a piece is to be played. Likewise, social characteristics affect individual orientations and actions, e.g. the way the orchestra and its governing board are organized affecting the individual musicians' morale, which in turn influences their motivation to cooperate and perform.

Our interest at this point in the analysis, therefore, is to change the focus from the individual level of analysis to that of structural and cultural factors. We want to identify social factors that affect the levels of church members' resistance to women in ministry.

DENOMINATIONAL DIFFERENCES IN RECEPTIVITY

The first set of comparisons to be discussed are
those involving denominational differences in resistance
to women in ministry. The four denominations included in
the study certainly have unique histories, cultural
traditions, organizational structures, systems of
theology, and so forth. They sometimes stress divergent
views on the nature of the church, the concept of the
ordained ministry, and the relationships between church
and society. The question here is whether any such
denominational differences carry over to their members'
attitudes towards the ordination and installation of women
as Christian ministers.

The figures contained in Table 5.1 include the
rankings of the four religious bodies in terms of the five
aspects of receptivity/resistance which apply to all four
groups. Those dimensions, once again, are perceptions of
women's general reliability, perceptions of their ability
to manage role conflict, preferences for men or women in
liturgical roles and in organizational functions, and
final willingness to accept a woman as one's minister.

The data in Table 5.1 reveal a fairly consistent
pattern of relationships between denominational
affiliation and resistance to clergywomen. Regardless of
the dimension under consideration, Anglicans and Baptists
tend to be the more conservative grouping, and Methodists
and United Reformed members tend to be the more receptive
pair. The differences between the Anglicans and Baptists
are slight, as are the divergences between Methodists and
United Reformed. The differences in receptivity between
the pairs of denominations tend to be consistently large.

Accordingly, the denominational labels are indeed
predictive of differences in resistance to women in

Table 5.1

CORRELATIONS (GAMMA) BETWEEN MEASURES OF RELIGIOUS SEXISM
AND SELECTED CLASSIFICATIONS OF DENOMINATIONS#

	rank-order* of denominations by receptivity	rank-order@ of sect/church types by receptivity	type of church polity	time since approved clergywomen
reliability stereo score	B/A/M/U	S/C/M	ns**	-.12
role conflict stereo score	B/A/M/U	S,C/M	ns	-.10
sacramental pref. score	B/A/M/U	S/C/M	ns	-.14
organizational pref. score	B/A/M/U	S/C/M	ns	-.06
will accept qualified woman	B/A/U/M	S/C/M	.18	.38

* "A" = Anglicans; "B" = Baptist; "M" = Methodist; "U" = United Reformed

** statistically non-significant relationship

Persons wishing detailed information on the rank-orderings reported here may obtain them by writing the author.

@ "S" = sect; "M" = mixed; "C" = church. Rates determined by percent above the median.

ministry. The evidence is both consistent and clear. We now ask why those patterns emerged. What is it about being "Anglican" or "Baptist" that results in greater resistance to clergywomen? What is unique to being "Methodist" or "United Reformed" that produces greater receptivity to women clergy? To answer these questions, we turn to a number of conceptualizations of the denominations which have long been a part of sociological thought about religious groups -- types of church polity, church/sect theory, dominant ideology, and social class composition. To them we also add the simple notion of how long the denomination has endorsed the ordination of women.

Receptivity/Resistance and Church Polity

The term "church polity" refers to the ways in which denominations and congregations govern themselves. They do not all do this in the same way (for a review of these concepts, see Chalfant, et al, 1981, pp. xxx-xxx). The three major types of church polity are the "episcopal," the "presbyterial," and the "congregational." These terms do not refer only to specific denominations bearing similar formal names, but instead denote types of structures for governing church life.

The "episcopal" type is basically hierarchical with authority and power centralized at the level of the broad denomination as a whole. Current examples of this mode of church governance include the Roman Catholic Church, the Mormons, and the Salvation Army. Decisions affecting policy are reserved to those atop the hierarchy, and the people in the pews have little authority and power.

At the opposite extreme is the "congregational" type. In this instance the church's authority and power reside in the local congregation. Each local church is defined as an autonomous gathered community of believers who make their own policy decisions under the presumed guidance of God and without any interference from denominational officials. The denominational level is considered an organizational convenience for cooperation of like-minded congregations, and it has no official power over those local bodies. An example of this type of structure in the United States is the Southern Baptist Convention.

In between these extremes is the "presbyterial" type. Its ideal for power and authority is neither completely centralized nor decentralized. Instead, this type of structure involves intermediate representative assemblies where policies governing local congregations are determined. It is a federated system involving checks and balances on power. An example today is the Presbyterian Church (U.S.A.).

Some persons who have studied these forms of religious organization have argued that they make a difference in the ability of individuals and congregations to address various issues and implement their own decisions. Such differences in power and authority also imply an ability to enforce ideologies and to insist on homogeneous belief systems. The types imply homogeneity of thought and attitudes in the hierarchical structures and greater divergence of thought in the decentralized types. Is this the case concerning members' attitudes towards women in ministry?

To assess the usefulness of this mode of thinking for understanding differences in attitudes towards clergywomen, we classified the four denominations in terms of the type of church polity they represented most closely. The Church of England is officially "episcopal" in their polity, while the Baptists tend to be the most "congregational." The Methodists are slightly less hierarchical than the Anglicans, and the United Reformed Church is a bit less congregational than the Baptists.

Thus we classified the four denominations in order from most hieirarchical to most congregational -- the Anglicans, then Methodists, followed by United Reformed and finally Baptists. We then compared the results of these classifications to the members' various sexism scores, and the results of those correlations are contained in Table 5.1. If differences in polity as defined by the categories listed above account for differences in attitudes towards clergywomen, then we should find a linear relationship between the typological classifications and each dimension of religious sexism.

As you can see, the polity classifications were significantly associated with differences in receptivity on only one dimension -- willingness to accept a qualified woman. The "congregational" end of the continuum was more associated with acceptance of clergywomen than was the "episcopal" type. But there were no such differences in terms of stereotyping or preferring men or women in clergy roles. Furthermore, the one relationship between polity and willingness to accept a woman as minister was actually more <u>curvilinear</u> than linear, with the very highest receptivity indicated among the United Reformed and the Methodists. Thus the "polity" approach to denominational differences in sexism was not very useful.

Receptivity and the Church/Sect Dichotomy

Another way of classifying religious bodies is in terms of the "church/sect" typology. This type of conceptualization derives from the work of Max Weber as developed and popularized by his student and interpreter

Ernst Troeltsch (1931). Perhaps the most thorough recent treatment of the scheme is that of Yinger (1970) as he refined the concepts themselves and extended the dichotomy to include other types, such as the "denomination" in pluralistic societies.

Basically Troeltsch (1931), looking mostly at the European historical scene, viewed Christian religious groups in one of two categories -- as either "churches" or "sects." The church type was seen as a large, dominant religious group composed of well-to-do members, with large financial and other economic resources, a trained clergy, and a formal liturgy, and which was institutionalized as the official religious system of the society. The sect type, by way of contrast, was a small, schismatic group dissenting from the characteristics of the dominant church, composed of less affluent members, with few economic resources, less insistence on an educated clergy, an informal and emotionally charged liturgy, and which was suffering social disadvantages as a deviant religious system. Again, while other types have been added to the scheme (e.g. Yinger, 1970), these differences still tend to dominate many observers' thinking about religious groups -- as "church" types or as "sect" types.

The question for this analysis is whether the church/sect typology is useful for explaining differences in religious sexism. Church-type groups are supposed to contain a higher proportion of educated members who are happy to compromise their religious beliefs and practices in the name of pragmatic social and political agendas. And members of sects are purportedly more insistent on retaining the letter of the pristine faith, unwilling to compromise in the name of power, prestige or social convenience. If the scheme is applicable to the issue of religious sexism in contemporary society, then members of the church type should manifest the greatest receptivity to women in ministry, and members of the sect type should manifest the greatest resistance to clergywomen.

To pursue this line of reasoning, we classified the four groups in the study in terms of the church/sect dichotomy. The history of relations between the religious bodies and political and economic institutions in England clearly resembles points in Troeltsch's thought. Today the Church of England is still the official State Church, and it rejects the label "Protestant," thus identifying with the long churchly tradition of the Roman Catholic Church. And the Baptists, Methodists, and United Reformed churches in England often still carry the label of the "Free Churches" in contrast to the Anglicans who retain ties to the central government.

Officially the British situation today is a pluralistic one, with no sanctions applying to dissenting religious groups. But the four denominations do differ in the extent to which they embody other characteristics of the church and sect types. Thus there is widespread consensus that the Church of England should be classified as a "church" type. There is also agreement that the Baptists usually represent a "sect" type of group. The Methodists and Presbyterians represent neither type very well, so we classified them as "mixed" or "intermediate" types of groups. They contain fewer church-type characteristics than the Church of England, and they contain less sect-like qualities than the Baptists. So we classified the four denominations in those terms.

The results of comparing the church/sect classifications with the measures of resistance to women in ministry are shown in Table 5.1. We ranked the types in terms of the proportion of members having resistance scores above the median on each dimension of sexism. The results are not consistent with what one would predict on the basis of church/sect thinking. The most sect-like group does tend to be the most resistant to clergywomen, but it is followed quite closely by the most church-like body. The two mixed types turn out to be the most accepting of women in ministry. So the conceptualizations of religious groups embodied in the church/sect typology are not predictive of differences in religious sexism in a way that is consistent with the rationale of the typology.

Receptivity and Social Class Composition

Another fact of life for many religious bodies is the social strata from which they draw most of their members. Historically the "masses" of ordinary people have tended to be at least under-represented in (if not alienated from) the socially legitimated churches in European societies (e.g. Pin, 1964). The dominant state churches in Europe historically have been operated by the dominant social classes and have catered largely to their interests. In the United States, each denomination manifests fairly clear tendencies for drawing its members from an identifiable band of strata in the status hierarchy (for a review of these patterns, see Chalfant, et al, 1981: 371-412). Episcopalians, for example, tend to be upper-middle-class people, while members of various Holiness and Pentecostal churches are predominantly from blue-collar families.

These modalities in the status composition of religious groups affect many aspects of their collective life -- how they are organized, the kind of religious leadership they have, the characteristics of their public ritual, the type of church music they sing and hear, their goals as churches, the nature of their church buildings, etc. Such patterns could also affect their shared orientations to the idea of women in ministry.

We have already shown in Chapter 3 that some of these differences in socio-economic status are related to some variations in religious sexism. Members in high-income brackets, those with high levels of formal education, and persons in high-status occupations tended to manifest less resistance to clergywomen than members with the opposite sets of status characteristics.

The question at this point is whether the four denominations in the study are systematically differentiated from each other in terms of the social strata from which most of their members come. If the different religious bodies tend to draw their members from specific social strata, then the denominational differences in resistance to women in ministry noted above could be due in part to those status differences.

I anticipated the possible significance of denominational status differences from the beginning of the study. As an American I also brought certain biases to the issue. Basically I expected American patterns to apply to England as well. Since American Episcopalians are a part of the broader Anglican tradition, for example, I expected members of the Church of England to manifest the same relatively high status as members of the Episcopal church in the United States. Similarly, I expected British Baptists to be drawn from a relatively low band of social strata, since the Baptists tend to be drawn from lower classes in the United States.

However, during informal consultations with British survey researchers prior to data collection, I was reminded of the dangers of making such hasty assumptions. Various British colleagues argued that the American pattern would not be found in England. Nevertheless, the predictions they themselves made of the status characteristics of English churches enjoyed no consensus at all. One observer expected the Baptists to manifest the highest status and the Anglicans the lowest. Another argued that the United Reformed Church would emerge as the group with the most high-status members and that the Anglicans would be somewhere in the middle.

To check out this situation empirically, we reviewed the status characteristics of the four denominations. We compared them in terms of their members' education, occupation, and income. The results were such as to call "a pox on all our houses!" There were no statistically significant differences in the status composition of the four denominations in the study. They all tended to draw from the full spectrum of variations in education, occupation, and income. Accordingly, it is not possible to explain denominational differences in resistance to women in ministry in terms of their unique status characteristics. It appears as though there are none.

Sexism and Predominant Theology

A fourth approach to explaining the denominational variations in resistance to clergywomen is in terms of the kinds of theological emphases which predominate in each group. We observed in Chapter 3 that individual members who placed high emphasis on traditional evangelism also tended to oppose women in ministry, while persons who stressed the social reform role of the church tended to favor the ordination of women. If it can be shown that such specific theological preferences also tend to characterize denominations as a whole, i.e. that there is widespread consensus about such priorities denomination-wide, then perhaps the denominational patterns of resistance to clergywomen will prove to be mainly a matter of theology.

To assess this possibility, we compared the denominations in terms of the relative emphasis their members placed on traditional evangelism and on social reform. As for evangelism, as a group the Baptists tended to stress soul-winning the most, while the Anglicans preferred that orientation the least. The Methodists and United Reformed fell in between these extremes (p<.0001). As one would predict in view of this pattern, it was the Anglicans who valued social reform the most highly, the Baptists the least, and the Methodists and United Reformed in between (p<.0001). Accordingly, while denominational modalities are apparent, it is also clear that they do not account for any of the denominational differences in receptivity to clergywomen, because the Anglicans and Baptists share the resistant extreme in terms of sexism, while they are at opposite poles in terms of theological emphasis.

Sexism and Date of Denominational Endorsement

The final approach to explaining the denominational differences in resistance to clergywomen to be considered here relates back to the historical developments reviewed in Chapter 1. It deals simply with the order in which the various bodies endorsed the ordination of women as clergy. Recall that the first group to accept the idea was the Congregationalists, who later became the United Reformed Church through merger with the Presbyterians. The second body officially to approve of women in ministry was the Baptists. The Methodists had endorsed the concept most recently. And, of course, the Church of England had not sanctioned women's ordination as of this writing.

A comparison of the rankings of the denominations on resistance to clergywomen on the one hand and timing of endorsement on the other reveals another curvilinear pattern, one with two sets of peaks and valleys. However, the results of calculating rank-order correlations between the two variables did produce some consistent linear statistics. As shown in Table 5.1, there is a significant linear correlation between timing and each dimension of resistance to women in ministry. The linear coefficients indicate that the longer the time that had elapsed since endorsing women's ordination, the more receptivity there was among its lay members.

These relationships are as intriguing as they are irregular. In view of the curvilinear association between the rankings, it is possible that the significant coefficients are but epiphenomenal of some accidental "roller-coaster" pattern in the rankings of denominational levels of receptivity when ordered by date of endorsement. However, it is possible that the length of time an official policy about women in ministry has been in place has some effect on the attitudes of the lay members. We have no way of determining the answer to these questions with the data in hand. The issue must await an historical analysis at some future date.

Summary

When church members' levels of receptivity to women in ministry were broken down by denomination, at least two clear and consistent patterns emerged. Members of the Church of England and of the Baptist Union tended to be more resistant to the idea, while members of the United Reformed Church and the Methodist Church were more receptive.

The analysis then compared a series of categorizations of denominations to levels of receptivity to clergywomen. The denominational breakdowns were based on the logic of five different criteria derived from as many theoretical approaches to understanding differences between religious groups. The theories dealt with church polity, the church/sect dichotomy, social class composition, theological climate, and date of official denominational endorsement of the ordination of women.

The results indicated that none of these conceptual schemes explained denominational differences in resistance to clergywomen with any consistency. Incidentally, the results did not change significantly with the introduction of controls. We controlled for the social class and theological orientation in the relationships between the measures of resistance to clergywomen and both the church/sect classifications and the polity breakdown. The partials closely resembled the zero-order coefficients.

This result should not be interpreted as indicating that the conceptual approaches themselves are intrinsically flawed. They have produced too many useful insights in other investigations to justify any such conclusion. These results simply tell us that, regardless of their utility in other contexts, the theories were not useful in explaining denominational differences in religious sexism in England in 1984. Denominational variations in attitudes towards women in ministry remain to be explained in the context of future studies.

SEXISM AND CONGREGATIONAL DIFFERENCES

Another set of social factors that may be useful for explaining variations in church members' resistance to women in ministry is the differences in characteristics of their local congregations. It is possible that women ministers would work out better in some types of local churches than in others.

I asked church officials and laypersons about this idea during the preparatory stages of the study. Where did they think women clergy would be more acceptable than elsewhere? The answers revealed little consensus on most points. Some members said women would be more welcome in large churches, because at times they needed multiple staff. Of course, this reply nearly always assumed that the woman would be in one of the subordinate clergy positions in such a church -- not the senior minister! Others replied that women clergy would be more acceptable in small congregations, because such churches did not require the maturity and experience which mainly men could bring. (!@#*?!)

Another type of reply focused not on the church itself but instead on its locale. Some members said that women would work out better in urban churches where there would be other professional women nearby to serve as a type of support group for the clergywoman. Others argued that women ministers would be more acceptable in rural areas, because there would be fewer demands on them from a smaller congregation.

The one major point of similarity in many of the replies was that "women ministers would work out better in churches which are different from mine!" City dwellers asserted that women are best suited for work in rural parishes. Rural folk said women clergy would fit best in urban churches. Members of small congregations argued that large parishes would have the best place for women ministers, while people in large churches indicated that the demands of small congregations are more suited to the energies and unique qualities women could provide. There were exceptions to this pattern, of course, but those were the typical responses.

So, what about it? Do people in different types of church also vary systematically in the level of their receptivity/resistance to women in ministry? We tried to anticipate this question by asking the pastors of the churches in the survey about some characteristics of their parishes. We collected this information from the ministers, because we assumed that on balance we would obtain more accurate information about the parish as a whole from them than from the lay members.

The results of correlating congregational differences with measures of resistance to women in ministry are contained in Table 5.2. The figures indicate that some congregational differences are indeed predictive of variations in sexism.

Resistance and Church Size

The first variable to be considered was church size. Research in the United States (e.g. Lehman, 1985; 98) has shown that size of congregation is related to receptivity to women in ministry. The larger the congregation, the more resistant the members were to women clergy. The data in Table 5.2 indicate that the same situation exists among church members in England. Members of large congregations tended to manifest higher scores on stereotyping and gender preferences, and displayed less willingness to accept a qualified woman pastor, than those in smaller churches. Differences in church size were not predictive of different attitudes towards women as deacons and women ordained abroad, however.

On the one hand, it would seem reasonable to argue that larger churches have more resources for undertaking new ventures which involve possible risk, and that this would lead their members to be more willing to consider the idea of women in ministry. They certainly would seem to have human and economic capital as to give them flexibility to undertake new ventures. However, just the opposite was the case. The greater receptivity to women clergy was displayed by members of the smaller churches.

Resistance and Congregational Trends

Another way of approaching the effects of church size is in terms of trends in membership over time rather than absolute size at the time of the study. One study in the United States (Lehman, 1979) indicated that membership trends were related to attitudes towards clergywomen. Members of growing and stable churches tended to be more opposed to women in ministry than those in declining congregations.

We asked the ministers whether their congregations were growing, holding their own, or declining in relation to trends in the population of the surrounding community. The correlations in Table 5.2 indicate that variations in their answers were systematically associated with differences in resistance scores in the same way as was observed in the American study. Members of growing churches tended to stereotype clergywomen, to prefer men in clergy roles, and to reject qualified women candidates more than those in declining congregations.

We asked a similar question concerning the trend of the congregation's budget. We asked the pastors whether, in comparison to inflation, the church budget was growing, holding its own, or declining. Evidence from two studies in the United States (Lehman, 1979; 1985) had shown that budget trend was related to receptivity to clergywomen in

Table 5.2

CORRELATIONS (GAMMA) BETWEEN MEASURES OF RECEPTIVITY/RESISTANCE TO WOMEN IN MINISTRY AND SELECTED CONGREGATIONAL CHARACTERISTICS AMONG PROTESTANT LAY CHURCH MEMBERS IN ENGLAND

	size of congregation	membership trend	budget trend	multiple affiliations
reliability stereotyping score	ns*	.11	.07	ns
role conflict stereotyping score	.10	.15	.13	ns
sacramental gender preference score	.10	.15	.10	ns
organizational gender preference score	.07	.10	ns	ns
will accept qualified woman	-.25	-.24	-.16	.27
FREE CHURCHES ONLY:				
willingness to discriminate	.09	.11	.11	ns
ANGLICANS ONLY:				
reject women as deacons	ns	ns	ns	ns
reject women ordained abroad	ns	ns	ns	ns

* indicates a statistically non-significant correlation.

much the same as membership trend was. Once again, the
evidence in Table 5.2 indicates that members of
prosperous congregations tended to be more opposed to
clergywomen than those in struggling churches.

Sexism and Multiple Affiliations

The final congregational difference we examined dealt
once again with denominational affiliation, i.e. whether
the congregation had multiple denominational affiliations.
(Again, these data were obtained from the local minister.)
Some congregations, for a variety of historical and
ideological reasons, elect to align themselves with more
than one parent body. For example, some local churches
identify themselves with both the Baptist Union and the
United Reformed Church. Others are affiliated with both
the Church of England and the Methodist Church. We
suspected that congregations with sufficient liberality to
associate with more than one denomination would also
manifest relatively high levels of receptivity to women in
ministry.

However, that expectation was borne out in only one
correlation between multiple affiliation and receptivity.
Dually aligned churches tended to be more willing to
accept a qualified woman as pastor than churches
cooperating with but one denomination (see Table 5.2).
There was no relationship between multiple affiliation and
other dimensions.

Implications of Congregational Correlates

The relationships between resistance to clergywomen
and congregational size, membership trend, and budget

trend imply a rather pragmatic rationale for some of those attitude differences. That is, the pattern of members in small and marginal churches approving women's ordination, while those in large and prosperous churches oppose it, suggests the operation of some simple labor market forces. Members of "fat-cat" churches do not have to take women in ministry seriously. Those churches probably can get along quite well without them.

By contrast, members of declining and struggling bodies, situations to which it is difficult to attract competent clerical leadership, often find themselves confronting the very real prospect of having to choose between modifying their requirements for a minister on the one hand, and closing the church doors on the other. Given the emotional attachments which many church members have to their local parish, it is not surprising that the sentiments to keep the doors open are stronger than the preferences for traditional male clergy. Thus it is not surprising to find members of marginal congregations more willing than those in prosperous churches to be open to the idea of having women in roles of professional church leadership.

SUMMARY

In this chapter we switched from the individual to the social level of analysis. We were concerned to see whether differences in denominational affiliation and congregational characteristics were predictive of variations in the prevalence of religious sexism among lay church members.

Comparisons of measures of resistance to women in ministry with denominational differences revealed a set of consistent patterns. On all dimensions of attitudes--

stereotyping, gender preferences, and readiness to accept qualified women as pastors -- members of Anglican and Baptist churches tended to be the most resistant to clergywomen. People belonging to the Methodist Church and the United Reformed Church were predominantly receptive to women as clergy.

In an effort to understand why such denominational patterns emerged from the analysis, we classified the denominations according to conceptual schemes derived from several theories about differences in religious groups. In this vein we examined the denominational patterns in the light of differences in church polity, the church/sect typology, social class composition, dominant theology, and time since denominational endorsement of the ordination of women. None of these approaches proved adequate to account for denominational differences in sexism.

It just may be that the quality of denominational leadership with regard to this issue is the determining factor. Where church leaders perceive the significance of an issue and develop programs to nudge the laity to learn new perspectives on it, their actions should result in attitudinal differences in comparison to religious bodies where the leadership either does nothing or takes the opposite approach. Unfortunately, we do not have data with which to assess this approach, and it must await future research of a historical nature.

Finally, we compared differences in characteristics of the members' local congregations with variations in resistance to women in ministry. Three congregational factors proved to be predictive of the prevalence of religious sexism, i.e. church size, membership trend, and budget trend. Members of large, growing, and affluent congregations tended to be more resistant to women in ministry than those in small and struggling churches.

The consistency of the correlations between church characteristics and measures of resistance to clergywomen suggest the impact of members' concern over the future of their congregations. Where the future viability of the church was at stake, it seems, more members were willing to consider accepting women in ministry as a viable option for their church leadership.

We pursue this avenue of thought more fully in the next chapter, where we consider the impact of members' concerns for the organizational viability of their congregations on their orientations to women in ministry.

CHAPTER 6
SEXISM AND PROBLEMS OF
ORGANIZATIONAL MAINTENANCE

One of the patterns to emerge from the preceding analysis is that members of large, growing, and prosperous churches manifested more religious sexism than those in small churches with declining membership rolls and shrinking budgets. People in struggling congregations were more receptive to women in ministry than those in stable situations.

Such generalizations make sense when one considers the organizational consequences of variations in church size and resources, not the least of which is the quality of church leadership one is able to obtain in the person of the minister or parish priest. Whether by a call from the local congregation or by an appointment from the central denominational offices, the best talent typically goes to the large, flourishing churches, and the least qualified leaders go to the least promising charges. The practice is as widespread in the Western world as it is paralleled in other segments of the natural order. It is no less curious from the perspective of Christian ethics.

The linkage between the organizational strength of the congregation and its members' attitudes towards women in ministry is probably a simple artifact of labor market forces. People in strong, affluent churches have virtually all of the resources they think they need. In such a situation, they have little pressure on them to take the idea of women in ministry seriously. They can ignore the entry of women into the clergy ranks. They do not need to consider any possible departure from past practices, because they have no trouble getting the calibre of church leadership they want.

Members of struggling congregations, on the other

hand, frequently find themselves faced with the prospect of disbanding. If they cannot muster the resources with which to mount a meaningful church program, especially if the situation involves their inability to support a parish priest or a full-time pastor, one option which they must face repeatedly is that of closing the church doors. Other ways of adapting to such scarcity are to look to part-time leadership, perhaps in the person of a retiree, to depend on lay leadership, or to use the services of clerical novices in the process of ministerial training.

When the concept of women clergy is introduced into this kind of situation, it presents yet another way of solving the leadership problem. Instead of having either to disband the congregation, do without a minister, or be content with sub-standard leadership, the entry of women into the ministry presents these members of marginal churches with at least the prospect of obtaining full-time, talented, and otherwise qualified ministerial services once again. Thus the members of marginal churches would be expected to manifest less religious sexism than those in prospering congregations, even though the latter have more organizational resources with which to adapt to change.

THE ORGANIZATIONAL MAINTENANCE DYNAMIC

At the heart of this way of thinking about church viability and members' willingness to consider women in ministry is a set of assumptions about how church members relate to their local congregations. Some parishioners identify strongly with their church. They are concerned about its welfare and its future, they are sensitive to things that would either promote or retard its well-being, and they are prepared to act to enhance its viability.

Other members, on the other hand, do not so identify with their congregation. It is not important to them. They do not take note of events that would affect the church, and they are not particularly anxious to do anything to ward off the effects of things that could hurt the congregation. The former type of member has internalized a set of norms related to the maintenance of the viability of the congregation, whereas the second type has not. This difference in members' orientation to their church can influence the ways in which they relate to church programs and to a variety of issues churches confront. In this chapter we shall examine the effects of these orientational differences on attitudes towards women in ministry.

Norms of Organizational Maintenance

As I have argued elsewhere (Lehman, 1981b; 1985), some differences in religious sexism can be explained within this frame of reference of church members wishing to protect and enhance the viability of their local congregation. Even though churches and other religious bodies are theological communities, they are also human organizations which have common social characteristics irrespective of their theological ethos. Organizations have attributes that differentiate them from other social forms (Etzioni, 1964; Katz and Kahn, 1970). Since most of the current feminist challenge to the male-dominated ministry is taking place almost exclusively within such organizational structures, it is possible that conceptualizing some barriers to women in ministry in organizational terms will help us understand receptivity and resistance more fully.

People create formal organizations as a way of

accomplishing a variety of things they want to do -- to manufacture articles for sale, to govern their collective life as communities, to facilitate their desires for leisure activities, and so forth. Organizations are but rather complex means for attaining a variety of goals.

Regardless of the specific goals which led to the creation of various organizations, they tend to share several characteristics in common. One such trait common to formal organizations is that they seem to develop their own sets of requirements once they are in existence, needs which tend to subordinate other aspects of organizational life (Etzioni, 1964: 5). We are interested in one of those requirements, i.e. the necessity of protecting the viability of the organization qua organization if people's goals are to continue to be met through the organization. This need for organizational maintenance seems prima facie to be a universal defining characteristic of organizations as such. It is apparently widely accepted as legitimate by most members within them (Katz and Kahn, 1970; 99). Members usually act as though they think the organization should be protected from disruptive influences.

Some observers have argued that the operation of this "maintenance dynamic" is a matter of people implementing norms which enhance the organization's competitive position in relation to resources it needs to remain viable (Seashore and Yuchtman: 1967). Chief among such resources of organizations qua organizations are access to people and those individuals' compliance with organizational role expectations. Without access to the first resource -- people -- there is no organization. Without compliance with organizational norms, the unit could cease to exist altogether.

Meeting these organizational requirements tends to be more difficult for churches than for secular organizations, especially in the area of access to resources necessary for their maintenance. This is true, first of all, because religious organizations-- especially local congregations -- are voluntary organizations. Protecting the organizational viability of voluntary associations is more difficult than is the case with non-voluntary structures (Hall, 1977:226 et passim). Participation in voluntary associations is what Etzioni (1964:65-67) calls "moral" rather than "coercive." All organizations must influence the lives of their members. In order to exercise such social control, members (especially leaders) of voluntary associations must convince other members to think and act in accordance with organizational norms. They cannot really coerce compliance. Members who are not convinced to conform can simply withdraw their participation from the organization. Voluntary associations typically live under these twin threats of deviance and defection of members.

Associated with this principle is a second consideration uniquely applicable to churches, and that is the relative absence of any serious consequences of not participating in them. This observation is what some investigators (e.g., Katz and Kahn, 1970: 121) call the "low potency" of religious involvements, i.e. how little difference they tend to make in terms of immediate consequences. Most work organizations and some political associations have quite high levels of "potency," because they actually control so many basic rewards that are empirically apparent to the participants. To comply brings relatively immediate reward, and to refuse to participate usually brings clear negative consequences. Not so for the churches. Members can "take it or leave it" with few immediate consequences, especially in societies where religion has been greatly privatized.

This problem is exacerbated by a third characteristic of churches in most Western societies, i.e. their having no monopoly on defining the normative aspects of life, particularly the religious situation (e.g., Berger, 1969; see also Etzioni, 1964: 74). Religious organizations have to compete with each other and with secular structures to get people to lend credence to their message and to heed its call. As modern consciousness has proceded to capture the mental outlook of Westerners, the churches have tended to lose out to secular forces in that competition, and the traditional "mainline" churches have experienced more organizational and programmatic erosions than sects and cults with mass appeal.

It is into that congeries of factors that the women-in-ministry issue has been placed. Leaders of some denominations have reacted to the movement for women's ordination with enthusiastic support. They have worked for changes in denominational policy which would affirm the women's sense of call and would facilitate their movement into various positions in ministry. Similarly, many laypersons at the local church level endorse the concept of women's ordination, while others oppose it.

Nevertheless, <u>even some church members who endorse the ordination of women in principle resist its implementation at the level of the congregation.</u> The source of their opposition lay in their perceptions of the organizational consequences of the change, especially their expectation that installing women as pastors and priests will result in some members withdrawing from church participation, withholding economic resources, or deciding to withdraw from that church and become members of another congregation or even another denomination. They are afraid that pushing the women-in-ministry issue will create problems of organizational maintenance.

Evidence from the United States

In previous work dealing with the organizational maintenance motif and religious sexism, the empirical evidence seemed to support the argument presented above. Analysis of survey data from national samples of church members in two Protestant denominations in the United States showed linear relationships between indicators of concern for organizational viability and resistance to women in ministry (Lehman, 1981b; 1985). Members who perceived that the introduction of a woman's candidacy into their search for a new minister would lead to conflict in the congregation, loss of members, reduced church participation, or declines in financial contributions by other members were also more likely to stereotype clergywomen, to prefer a man in clergy roles, and to vote against women candidates than those who did not expect such declines. The influence of such expectations on receptivity to women in ministry was greatest when viewed in interaction with degree of commitment as manifest in ritual participation. Can these patterns be replicated in Britain?

Sexism and Organizational Maintenance in England

In order to evaluate the extent to which this approach to religious sexism also applies to church members in England, we included a series of items on the questionnaire to measure the variables associated with the organizational maintenance motif. We asked members of the Free Churches the following question:

"If the (appropriate search committee) recommended a woman as minister, do you think it would create tension or conflict in the congregation?"

The question posed to members of Anglican churches was slightly different, since their denomination had not yet endorsed women's ordination. They were asked whether the Church formally approving the entry of women into the priesthood would create tension or conflict in the congregation.

Combining these items, the overall response pattern showed that about 41 per cent of the members expected the introduction of women clergy into their congregation to result in internal dissension. Since the question asked of the Anglicans was slightly different from that posed to the members of the Free Churches, we also broke the responses down by denomination, and the results were as follows:

<u>percent perceiving discord</u>

Anglicans	55
Baptists	57
Methodists	29
United Reformed	26

As was the case with measures of sexism, the responses of the Anglicans and Baptists showed the highest proportions expecting tension, while the Methodists and United Reformed were similar in expecting less conflict. (This pattern also suggests that any apparent distinctiveness of the Anglicans on this issue is not due to the unique wording of the item.)

In addition to the above question dealing with discord in general, we also asked about possible specific organizational consequences of introducing the clergywoman issue to the congregation. Previous work, for example, has shown perceptions of declines in church participation to be a problem. To assess this possibility, we asked:

"If the church called a woman as minister, would you

expect some members of the congregation to stay away from church?"

About 39 per cent of the members indicated that some persons in the congregation would reduce their ritual involvement in church.

We also inquired about the possible impact of women in ministry on church finances:

"If the church called a woman, would you expect some members of the church to withhold their financial contributions?"

About 23 per cent indicated that their congregation's coffers would suffer in response to the introduction of women as possible ministers of their congregation.

Effects of Organizational Concerns on Sexism

If these concerns make any difference in members' attitudes towards clergywomen in England as they did in the United States, then differences in these expectations should be systematically related to the measures of receptivity/resistance to women in ministry. The correlations contained in Table 6.1 indicate that such is indeed the case. The associations between organizational concerns and religious sexism are clear and consistent. The more members expect the introduction of clergywomen into their congregation to result in general discord, in declines in church participation, and in reductions in financial contributions by other members, the more they manifest resistance to women in ministry -- they stereotype more, they prefer men in more clergy roles, they indicate that they will not accept a woman as their minister, they are prepared to discriminate against those women candidates, and among Anglicans they reject women as deacons and women ordained abroad.

Table 6.1 CORRELATIONS (GAMMA) BETWEEN MEASURES OF RECEPTIVITY/RESISTANCE TO WOMEN IN MINISTRY AND PERCEPTIONS OF ORGANIZATIONAL THREAT TO CONGREGATIONS, AMONG PROTESTANT LAY CHURCH MEMBERS IN ENGLAND

	expect tension or conflict	expect members to stay away from church	expect members withhold money	internalization of organizational norms
reliability score	.24	.22	.22	.20
role conflict score	.35	.35	.30	.17
sacramental score	.40	.36	.34	.20
organizational score	.24	.20	.23	.21
will accept qualified woman	.84	.67	.66	.34
FREE CHURCHES ONLY:				
willingness to discriminate	.34	.22	.25	.13
ANGLICANS ONLY:				
reject women as deacons	.60	.44	.55	.31
reject women ordained abroad	.70	.50	.57	.33

The same principle also seems to apply to the number of different ways in which members perceive possible organizational threats. If sexism is related to each type of potential threat to congregational viability, then it should also follow that the more of these negative outcomes they expect, the more sexist they will be.

We checked out this possibility by computing a "threat score" for each member. The score was calculated by simply giving each respondent one point for each way in which he/she thought clergywomen would have negative consequences for the church -- general conflict, reduced participation, and reduced giving. Persons who indicated a perception of threat on all three items received a score of "3." Those who saw threat on none of them had a score of "0," etc. The distribution of threat scores was as follows:

score	percent
0	51
1	16
2	15
3	19

About half of the members perceived no threat from women in ministry. Only a minority saw the congregation jeopardized in all three ways.

We then compared the members' "threat scores" with their indications of religious sexism, and the measures were consistently and clearly related. The more ways in which members perceived a threat to congregational stability, the more they also manifested resistance to women in ministry.

The correlations were as follows:

threat score

reliability stereotyping   .20
role conflict stereotyping .31
sacramental preferences   .34
organizational preferences .20
will accept clergywoman   .70
will discriminate   .25
reject women as deacons   .50
reject women ord. abroad   .56

Accordingly, as was the case in the United States, it is helpful to conceptualize the women-in-ministry issue in England in organizational terms, especially at the level of the local congregation. Local church attachments evidently can influence theological and normative judgements. Where members perceive negative consequences of women in ministry for their local congregation, these perceptions have a strong influence on their attitudes towards women in ministry in general.

Degree of internalizing organizational norms

An issue which earlier work in the United States (Lehman, 1981b; 1985) did not address, and one which has not been considered in this analysis up to now, is the extent to which individual church members had internalized norms of organizational maintenance. This is a potentially important omission, because it seems unlikely that all lay church members will have internalized such norms equally, regardless of their perceptions of possible organizational consequences of any issue. Just as members differ in the extent to which they accept religious beliefs and engage in ritual participation, it is likely that members also differ in the degree to which they have adopted the organizational perspective which says that congregational viability is to be protected and maintained.

Such differences in the internalization of norms of organizational maintenance are also likely to be related to differences in members' receptivity to women in ministry. The entry of women into the ordained ministry has almost universally been a controversial subject, especially in many local congregations into which the prospect of women clergy has actually been introduced. In line with the general perspective discussed in this chapter, it follows that members who have internalized norms of organizational maintenance would be more inclined to eschew such conflict and possible schism than members who have not adopted those organizational concerns. Thus operationally one would expect measures of internalizing organizational norms and of receptivity to women in ministry to be significantly related.

One would also expect that the relationship between internalizing the maintenance motif and receptivity to clergywomen would vary depending upon the extent to which members expect tension and conflict actually to break out. That is, level of receptivity to women in ministry should be a product of the <u>interaction</u> between actually perceiving organizational threat and internalizing norms of organizational maintenance. Members who have adopted such norms <u>and</u> perceive a woman's candidacy as creating conflict may be expected to oppose the introduction of female clerical leadership in their congregations. At the other extreme, those who perceive no threat <u>and have not</u> internalized organizational norms should be considerably less likely to oppose women in ministry. (In between these two extremes, the situation is less determinative.

Members who perceive organizational threat in a woman's candidacy, but who are not concerned about organizational viability, have less reason for opposing the introduction of female leadership than persons who perceive threat and have adopted organizational concerns. The same situation would apply to members who have internalized group norms but who perceive no threat in a woman's candidacy.)

Stated in yet another way, if it matters to an individual whether anything untoward happens to his or her church, then perceiving negative consequences of a woman minister will lead them to oppose her. By contrast, if it does not matter to a member whether the congregation has good or bad fortunes, then there is no reason for perceptions of negative congregational consequences of women in ministry to have any impact on attitudes towards clergywomen in general. "It's no skin off their nose."

By this reasoning, therefore, receptivity to women in ministry should be related to perceptions of organizational threat primarily in interaction with degree of internalization of organizational norms.

Internalizing norms and receptivity

We included an item on the questionnaire to measure the extent to which members had internalized norms of congregational maintenance. The question read:

"If some members stayed away from church or withheld contributions in response to a woman minister, how concerned would you be about the future of the congregation? Would it be:

very concerned (56%)

slightly concerned (28%)

not very concerned (11%)

not concerned at all (5%) ?"

It is apparent that many church members have internalized norms of organizational maintenance pertaining to their congregation. Over one-half say they would be "very concerned" if the church were threatened in this way. Only 16 per cent expressed little or no concern. The matter of congregational viability tends to be important to church members. At the same time, there were differences in response to the question, so we shall assume that we have in fact measured a variable and that we can compare the responses to other variables to check for possible relationships.

The final column in Table 6.1 contains the correlations between the measure of internalizing the organizational maintenance motif and measures of religious sexism. The coefficients proved to be in accordance with what one would predict on the basis of the above discussion. The more church members have internalized norms of congregational maintenance, the more they are opposed to women in ministry on all dimensions.

Interaction effects

The discussion of the maintenance motif also argued that differences in religious sexism would be related to degree of internalization of organizational norms primarily when members also perceive that a clergywoman in the role of pastor would promote dissension in the congregation. The same argument applies when you switch the independent and control variables, i.e. perceptions of threat will affect resistance to women in ministry primarily when the member also has internalized norms of congregational maintenance.

In order to assess this argument empirically, we correlated the indicators of resistance to clergywomen with the measure of internalizing organizational norms while controlling for perception of organizational threat. The partial correlations resulting from that analysis are contained in Table 6.2. Perception of "no threat" means that the respondents answered "no" to all of the items indicating that they thought clergywomen would threaten the viability of their congregation. The "threat" control category contains respondents who answered "yes" to any of those items.

The coefficients in Table 6.2 indicate that all measures of religious sexism were significantly related to internalization of norms of congregational viability among persons who also perceived that the presence of a clergywoman would create congregational problems. Among members who did not think the presence of a clergywoman would create discord in the congregation, most of the correlations were so small as to be statistically non-significant. The three coefficients that were statistically significant under this condition were clearly much smaller than the opposite situation. Thus it appears that it is the interaction between internalizing organizational norms and perceiving organizational threat which had the greatest impact on resistance to women in ministry.

The figures in Table 6.3 portray the results of switching the independent and control variables. It contains correlations between the three measures of member perceptions of organizational threat and the indicators of resistance to women in ministry, controlling for the degree of internalization of norms of organizational maintenance. ("High internalization" was indicated by members answering that they were either "very" or "slightly" concerned about the congregation. "Low" was indicated by the other two response categories.)

Table 6.2

CORRELATIONS (GAMMA) BETWEEN INTERNALIZATION OF NORMS OF ORGANIZATIONAL MAINTENANCE AND MEASURES OF RELIGIOUS SEXISM, CONTROLLING FOR PERCEPTION OF CONGREGATIONAL THREAT

	Perceive Threat	Perceive No Threat
reliability stereo score	.26	.17
role conflict stereo score	.28	.12
sacramental preference score	.36	ns*
organizational preference score	.30	.13
will accept qualified woman	.52	ns
FREE CHURCHES:		
willingness to discriminate	.29	ns
ANGLICANS:		
reject women as deacons	.31	ns
reject women ordained abroad	.28	ns

* statistically non-significant coefficient

Once again, the results support the notion that it is the <u>interaction</u> between perceiving threat and internalization of norms that most affects attitudes. For members who had indicated internalization of norms of organizational maintenance, indicators of all three measures of perceiving organizational threat were correlated with the measures of resistance to women in ministry. However, among those who had <u>not</u> internalized such norms, the relationships between measures of threat and of receptivity to clergywomen were either statistically non-significant or smaller than under the opposite condition. Only one of the twenty-four figures did not conform to this pattern.

It might be argued that these interaction effects are spurious in that one of the independent variables is epiphenomenal of the other. Specifically, one might assert that the measure of internalizing organizational norms produced answers which are but a reflection of members' perceptions of threats to congregational viability. If that were the case, then indeed such interaction effects would emerge from this kind of analysis. However, such is <u>not</u> the case in this instance. To check out this possibility, we compared the measure of internalizing norms to those indicating perceptions of threat, and the results were as follows:

	<u>internalization of norms</u>
create tension/conflict	.00
reduce participation	.08
reduce contributions	.03

None of these coefficients is statistically significant. So there is no contamination between the two sets of measures. We are dealing with true interaction effects.

Table 6.3

CORRELATIONS (GAMMA) BETWEEN PERCEPTIONS OF ORGANIZATIONAL THREAT AND MEASURES OF RELIGIOUS SEXISM, CONTROLLING FOR INTERNALIZATION OF NORMS

	HIGH DEGREE OF INTERNALIZATION			LOW DEGREE OF INTERNALIZATION		
	create tension	reduce attendance	reduce giving	create tension	reduce attendance	reduce giving
reliability score	.24	.24	.22	.22	ns*	.26
role conflict score	.38	.38	.35	ns*	.24	ns
sacramental score	.44	.42	.39	ns	ns	ns
organizational score	.25	.23	.24	ns	ns	ns
will accept woman	.86	.73	.71	.63	ns	ns
FREE CHURCHES:						
will discriminate	.40	.26	.32	ns	ns	ns
ANGLICANS:						
women as deacons	.59	.46	.54	.55	ns	ns
women ordained abroad	.67	.50	.56	.71	.26	ns

* statistically non-significant coefficient

Summary

Significant proportions of church members in England perceive the possibility that introducing a woman as minister of their congregation would create discord and threaten the viability of the community. Between about one-fourth and one-third of the church members said that if a woman were recommended as their pastor, there would either be tension and conflict in the congregation, some members would stay away from church, or some would withhold their financial contributions to the church. Any one of these possible consequences of introducing women in ministry constitutes a potential threat to congregational cohesiveness and longevity.

The analysis of the data indicated that measures of these perceptions were indeed related to indicators of religious sexism. Members who perceived such a threat were more opposed to women in ministry than were those who did not expect such consequences.

Similarly, a majority of the members said that they would be disturbed to some degree if the introduction of a clergywoman had such effects on their congregation. And people who had thusly internalized norms concerning church viability also tended to be significantly more opposed to clergywomen than were those who had not internalized those norms. These patterns indicate an organizational component to religious sexism, i.e. people's attitudes towards women as ordained clergy were partly an artifact of their attachments to their congregation and their perceptions of the effects of this kind of change in religious leadership.

Finally, the analysis also indicated that religious sexism is most affected by the interaction of these variables. That is, members who have internalized norms

to protect their church <u>and</u> who expect negative effects of
a woman minister on their congregation are the most likely
to be opposed to clergywomen. Where either of these
independent variables is not present, the effect of the
other is sharply attenuated.

ORGANIZATIONAL MAINTENANCE AND LOCALISM

When this organizational approach to explaining
resistance to women in ministry was introduced, some
observers wondered whether any empirical relationships
between the organizational maintenance motif and sexist
attitudes were actually spurious (e.g. McGuire, 1980).
According to this criticism, what appears to be resistance
based on church members internalizing norms of
organizational maintenance is actually an artifact of the
"localism" orientation discussed in chapter 4. The
supposed effects of concerns for congregational
maintenance would actually be due to the influences of
local/cosmopolitan orientations.

This suggestion is certainly worthy of serious
attention. After all, concerns for one's congregation are
clearly dealing with something "local." It is the
member's particular local church that is involved, not the
church universal. It just may be that expressions of
congregational concerns are just another manifestation of
cultural or ecclesiological localism.

At the time this suggestion surfaced, we had no data
with which to test the arguments empirically. However,
the British survey data do contain measures of all of the
variables involved, and we can use them to see which
perspective is supported by the evidence.

Recall that the analysis reported in earlier segments
of this volume indicated that religious sexism was

associated with both localism (chapter 4) and the congregational maintenance motif (above). These relationships appeared on virtually all dimensions of resistance to clergywomen.

The Question of Spuriousness

Are some of these relationships spurious? The original criticism of the organizational-maintenance theory of religious sexism asserted that the bivariate associations between sexism and organizational concerns are not valid. That is, the correlations between measures of the variables are considered as only artifacts of differences in members' local community attachments. If this is the case, then the correlations between sexism and organizational concerns should diminish significantly when the effects of localism are held constant.

However, the introduction of such controls into the analysis did not produce such results. Table 6.4 indicates the correlations between the church members' "threat" scores and the measures of resistance to clergywomen before and after the introduction of controls for the effects of cultural and ecclesiological localism. The results show that in no case did the control variable significantly alter the relationships. The partials are very close to the magnitude of the zero-order coefficients. Thus the initial relationships between measures of congregational concerns and the indicators of religious sexism were not spurious -- at least not explained away by this particular test factor.

The same pattern emerged when the relationships between sexism and localism were examined when controlling for the effects of the organizational maintenance motif. As shown in Table 6.5, the partial correlations were

Table 6.4

CORRELATIONS (GAMMA) BETWEEN THREAT SCORE AND MEASURES OF
RELIGIOUS SEXISM, CONTROLLING FOR CULTURAL AND
ECCLESIOLOGICAL LOCALISM

	zero-order relationship	Partial Correlations: control for cultural localism	control for eccl. localism
reliability stereo. score	.20	.23	.20
role conflict stereo. score	.31	.22	.31
sacramental pref. score	.34	.37	.35
organizational pref. score	.20	.22	.21
will accept woman	-.70	-.71	-.70
FREE CHURCHES:			
ready to discriminate	.25	.15	.25
ANGLICANS:			
reject women as Deacons	.50	.51	.48
reject ordained abroad	.56	.59	.51

virtually identical to the zero-order coefficients. Those relationships also appear not to be spurious.

These results are probably due to the absence of much of a relationship between the measures of perceiving organizational threat and localism. The correlations between those scores were as follows:

threat score

	threat score
cultural localism	-.10
ecclesiological localism	.00

There was no relationship between perceiving organizational threats and ecclesiological localism. But there was a weak <u>negative</u> correlation between threat score and cultural localism. The more church members viewed the world in narrow, localistic terms, the <u>less</u> likely they were to expect the introduction of a woman as their minister to lead to congregational problems. It is possible that this weak correlation is a result of sampling variation. (If it is not a statistical fluke, then I do not know what it implies.)

It is probably safe to assume at this point that, for all practical purposes, the effects of the organizational maintenance motif and of various dimensions of localism occur independently of each other. The congregational level of analysis and the perspective of local community perspectives and attachments are best conceived of as separate conceptual spaces when considering approaches to explaining differences in religious sexism.

SUMMARY

In this chapter we investigated the effects of identifying with one's congregation on religious sexism.

Table 6.5

CORRELATIONS (GAMMA) BETWEEN CULTURAL LOCALISM, ECCLESIOLOGICAL LOCALISM, AND
MEASURES OF RELIGIOUS SEXISM, CONTROLLING FOR PERCEPTIONS OF ORGANIZATIONAL THREAT

	cultural localism:		ecclesiological localism:	
	zero-order correlation	control for threat score	zero-order correlation	control for threat score
reliability stereo. score	.34	.35	.19	.20
role conflict stereo. score	.10	.12	.07	.08
sacramental pref. score	.21	.26	.19	.22
organizational pref. score	.28	.29	.21	.22
will accept woman	-.13	-.17	-.15	-.09
FREE CHURCHES:				
ready to discriminate	ns*	.12	ns	.08*
ANGLICANS:				
reject women as deacons	ns	.04*	ns	-.10*
reject ordained abroad	ns	.16*	ns	.06*

* statistically non-significant correlation

Some members are very concerned for the welfare of their local church. They want what is good for it, and they wish to avoid discord there. Others have no such personal investment in their congregation, and they lose little sleep over its future viability. These differences are manifestations of variations in the extent to which people have internalized "norms of organizational maintenance," patterns for thought and action which characterize virtually all formal associations and which emerge within them to insure the continued functioning of the organization in the future.

These organizational considerations are germane to the issue of women in ministry, because the emergence of clergywomen has been such a controversial matter. Church members often view the idea of women in ministry in such terms, and this perspective influences their readiness to endorse the concept.

The survey included measures of the extent to which the members had internalized such norms of congregational maintenance. A majority of members viewed their church in these terms. The questionnaire also contained indications of members' perceptions of the amount of threat that clergywomen would actually pose for their local church. Significant proportions thought that introducing clergywomen into their church would create problems in their congregation.

The analysis then indicated that the prevalence of religious sexism was related to the perceptions of women creating congregational problems and to their having internalized norms of organizational maintenance. The more that members expected the prospect of having a woman minister would alienate church members, the more they were opposed to women in ministry. Similarly, the more the members had internalized norms of congregational maintenance, the more they also resisted clergywomen in their churches.

It is important to note that these two variables--perceiving organizational threats and internalizing norms of organizational maintenance -- have their effects on attitudes towards women in ministry primarily in interaction with each other. Perceiving threats to the congregation by clergywomen affects attitudes towards women in ministry mainly if the person has also internalized the maintenance motif. Similarly, internalizing such norms will affect resistance to women in ministry if the member also expects the clergywomen issue to be disruptive to the congregation. The effects of the two variables are at least additive if not multiplicative.

Finally, the results of the analysis showed that these organizational factors are not reducible to differences in members' localism or vice versa. The local/cosmopolitan perspective and the organizational maintenance frame of reference appear to be quite separate from each other in their effects on religious sexism. They represent different levels of analysis and should not be confused with each other.

In the next chapter, we shift to yet another level of analysis, i.e. that of the total society. The indicators of many of the variables in this study are identical to those employed in similar research previously done in the United States. These parallels allow us to compare the results of the British study to those obtained in the American work to see whether there are any systematic differences in the ways in which British and American church members deal with the issue of women in ministry.

CHAPTER 7
BRITISH/AMERICAN COMPARISONS

Up to this point, the discussion of sexism in the churches has been restricted to the evidence obtained in the United Kingdom. The data we have examined was from a national-sample survey of church members in four denominations in England. These English church members differed widely in their receptivity/resistance to women in ministry. Some of those variations in sexism were attributable to individual differences in modern consciousness, localism, and identification with one's congregation. Other variations in resistance to clergywomen were due to differences in congregational and denominational characteristics.

SOCIETAL DIFFERENCES

In this chapter we move to the societal level of analysis. We compare the attitudes characteristic of the British scene to those previously observed in the United States, where nearly all of the empirical research on the women-in-ministry movement has been conducted to date (for a listing of most of this work, see Carroll, et al, 1983; and Lehman, 1985). Some of the American studies have made denominational comparisons (e.g. Jacquet, 1973 and 1977; and Carroll, et al, 1983), as well as the familiar breakdowns by socio-economic status, other background traits, congregational traits, etc. But to date there has been no empirical basis for comparing the American scene with patterns in other societies. With the present undertaking, we now have such a basis for comparison.

We shall be able to make British/American comparisons because the English study incorporated in the survey

instrument sets of questions which had been used
successfully in the work previously completed in the
United States. (We shall identify those specific items
below.) Not all of the items incorporated in the British
survey had such precedents, so we cannot do a comparative
analysis of all possible factors, but enough of them were
utilized in both studies to allow us to make at least a
beginning.

So the question we consider in this chapter is quite
straightforward -- do British and American church members
respond to the women-in-ministry movement in the same way?
If they do not, in what ways are they different, and why?

Arguments for Similarities Between Societies

Given what we think we know already about British and
American societies, what should we expect to find? There
are arguments both for and and against the idea that there
are notable differences between British and American
society, i.e. divergences sufficient to result in
detectable national variations in attitude towards women
in ministry. We cannot review them all here, for to do so
would require another volume. Instead we shall list a few
to illustrate at least some contrasting predictions.

In a methodological sense, one may legitimately
object that comparisons between the United States and the
United Kingdom hardly qualify as "comparative analysis."
After all, at least up through the eighteenth century, the
two societies participated in a common history, struggled
against the same enemies, developed similar political
values, etc. Still today they share numerous broad
cultural meaning systems and speak the same language.
These patterns hardly embody the range of social and
cultural variations the classical ethnographer would want

to have in hand before claiming to embark on a "comparative" study.

Similarly, many college curricula requiring students to complete one or more courses of non-Western studies as part of general education requirements do not allow any European studies to be applied to the requirement. From this perspective the US/UK comparison appears to be one of "apples and apples."

The classical societal typologies dealing with industrialization, urbanization, massification, etc., would also lead us to expect few important differences between the United Kingdom and the United States. Both societies have participated in roughly the same levels of industrialization and seem to be moving far into a post-industrial phase. They have experienced similar patterns of urbanization and have suffered equally with the social problems attendant on such mass concentrations. They have similar levels of literacy in their populations, and they have manifested like signs of being mass societies controlled by a few institutionally specific elites.

In view of both this sense of historical continuity and the classical models of comparative analysis we have in hand, then, how can one expect to observe any meaningful differences in religious institutions between two societies as similar as the United Kingdom and the United States? More specifically, these considerations would not lead one to expect wide differences between the two societies on the matter of receptivity or resistance to women in ministry.

Evidence of Historical Differences

However, in spite of these broad similarities between the two societies, others have argued that there are important differences between the United States and the United Kingdom, disparities which could contribute to societal variations in attitudes including orientations to the ordination of women.

Historian William Warren Sweet (1950), for example, discusses several important ways in which the American religious scene itself has been unique. First, according to Sweet the founders of the earliest Christian bodies in North America were political and religious radicals. They had been dissenters in Europe, and they came to the New World seeking escape from religious and political oppression -- which went together in those days. They were religious innovators, and their ideas were anathema to ruling groups in the Old World. They came to the New World explicitly to find a place in which they could exercise their own versions of the religious quest.

Second, the American religion they forged took shape in the context of a hostile frontier whose realities not only enhanced the new residents' wishes to be innovative but also virtually forced inventiveness on them if they were to survive. Well into the nineteenth century, the colonists and then Americans shaped and reshaped their institutions amid conditions of life encountered in frontier conditions. The rigors of conflict with the elements and hostile native Americans, coupled with the physical and cultural isolation from neighbors and other societies, not only helped to promote numerous innovations in politics and economics, but also furthered the development of new forms of religious life -- new structures of church polity, new modes of recruiting church leaders, new liturgical patterns, unique sacred music, etc.

A third factor that contributed to these innovations was the absence of an established religious system bolstered by law and other political sanctions. Without such restraints, the American church members were free selectively to accept, reject, modify, or invent religious patterns to their liking. One of the best examples of this unfettered religious inventiveness is revivalism, a ritual pattern still uniquely characteristic of the American religious scene. The theme is also illustrated in the steady proliferation of new religious and quasi-religious movements in the United States continuing well into the twentieth century.

Sweet also discussed other peculiarities of the American religious scene, such as the presence of black slaves and the high proportion of unchurched citizens, but let the above suffice for the moment. The major implication of these generalizations for us here is that religious institutions in the United States have participated in a broad ethos of innovation and willingness to depart from tradition. While it is doubtful that the concrete conditions which motivated people to develop unique religious institutions in the colonial period and the early years of the Republic will continue to direct their energies in similar directions in the twentieth century, it is nonetheless likely that those formative years established an American habit of mind which could at least allow if not facilitate other religious mutations today, innovations such as the ordination of women.

Other historians have pressed a similar point when discussing general differences between the United Kingdom and the United States, divergent themes not necessarily unique to religion but probably encompassing it. Snowman (1977), for example, suggests that one can identify broad value orientations which characterize one society more than the other, modalities which stand out in spite of many other ways in which each society is also quite heterogeneous. He discusses sets of values and myths which are more characteristic of the United States than the United Kingdom and others which are more British than American.

By far the most significant point Snowman (1977: 80-83) makes about the differences between British and American values and myths, however, involves the place that continuity and change have in them. American myths center on the foundation of something new, the origins of a new society, the great social experiment, the New World, the advent of religious freedom, motifs also noted by Bellah (xxxx) in his discussions of American civil religion. British myths, on the other hand, tend to emphasize continuity, successful resistance to potential disruptions from outside the society, and the defense and maintenance of the old ways. To the extent that the religious institutions participate in these distinctions, and it is difficult to see how they could avoid it, one may expect them to foster a greater willingness to consider religious change such as the ordination of women in America than in England.

Informal impressions gained from unstructured contacts with the citizens of each society also promote the expectation of differences between American and English religious devotees. One source of such perceptions is the jokes people share at informal social gatherings, on television talk shows, in the popular press, etc., stories which construct and reinforce negative stereotypes of members of the other society. Similarly revealing are the shared reactions to news stories about each other's country, especially where members of one society or the other are shown in situations which could lead their compatriots to be either proud or embarrassed.

An impression one picks up in these contexts is that members of the two societies sometimes perceive each other in these stereotypical and not always flattering terms, with images explicitly involving orientations towards stability and change. And there is no reason to expect church members to be exempt from such perceptual norms. Americans participate in a subculture containing perceptual habits which characterize the British as overly impressed with tradition, rigidly conservative, and a bit too stuffy socially -- all the while also being a bit envious of their long and dignified history. British people, for their part, share perceptions of Americans which portray them in equally unflattering terms, i.e. as uncultured, undisciplined, overly commercialized, and too willing to discard old cultural forms. And they, too, manifest some jealousy of the numerical and financial strength of American institutions including religious bodies. The people in each society _expect_ to see differences and thus expect also to _be_ different, and they feel ambivalence in relation to what they perceive.

Accordingly, both historical scholarship and unstructured observation suggest that we should not close the door prematurely to comparative analyses involving the United Kingdom and the United States. There are grounds for expecting both close similarities and broad differences. On any specific issue, therefore, the question of societal differences remains an empirical one, and this paper seeks to deal with the issue of church members' reactions to clergywomen in that mode.

NATIONAL SURVEY DATA

The opportunity to pursue these comparisons comes with the existence of parallel data from three national-

sample surveys, all of which focused on the responses of
lay church members to the ordination of women as
ministers. One of the surveys, of course, is the British
data set we have been examining in this volume. The other
two studies involve data collected in the United States
prior to the present undertaking. The first of these
American surveys was done among lay members of the
American Baptist Churches in 1978. As shown in Table 7.1,
the study yielded 424 replies for a response rate of about
85%. The second American data set is from the
Presbyterian Panel of April, 1980, (United Presbyterian
Church, USA), consisting of replies from 1720 lay members
and a response rate of 75%. Checks for non-response
bias in the surveys revealed minor discrepancies, but none
sufficiently great as to influence the analysis of the
women-in-ministry variables. This outcome is probably as
representative a set of samples as one is likely to get in
national survey research.

Table 7.1

PATTERNS OF RESPONSE TO SURVEYS OF CHURCH MEMBERS IN
SELECTED DENOMINATIONS IN THE UNITED STATES
AND THE UNITED KINGDOM

	Initial Sample	Returns	Response Rate
UNITED STATES:			
Baptist	500	424	85%
Presbyterian	2263	1720	75%
UNITED KINGDOM:			
Baptist	392	360	92%
United Reformed	375	358	95%

Data were collected in the same way in two of the investigations. The Presbyterian Panel in the United States involved a mailed questionnaire, as did the surveys of the English Baptists and the United Reformed Church members. The data from the American Baptists were collected by telephone interviews. (Persons wishing more details concerning the sampling and data collection may obtain it by contacting the author.)

We have in hand, then, data on attitudes towards women in ministry from two denominations in each of two societies. All four denominational groups have officially endorsed the ordination of women to the pastoral ministry (see Lehman, 1979; 1985). Some clergywomen are already placed as pastors of congregations in all four instances. The question now is whether there are observable national and denominational differences in religious sexism among their lay members.

Indicators of key concepts

In anticipation of possible comparative analysis, we used many of the same indicators of key variables in each survey. The wording of the questions was the same in each survey except for minor variations in terminology based on differences in denominational nomenclature. The result is that we have identical operationalizations of variables in studies of two denominations in each of two societies. This kind of data allows for clean comparisons across denominational and societal lines -- technically as uniform sets of data as one is likely to get.

The items shown in Table 7.2 constitute indicators of the three dimensions of attitudes towards clergywomen that we have examined in previous sections of this report, i.e. members' perceptions of what clergywomen are like,

Table 7.2 MEASURES OF RELIGIOUS SEXISM AMONG LAY CHURCH MEMBERS IN TWO DENOMINATIONS IN ENGLAND AND THE UNITED STATES

STEREOTYPING:	definitely true	probably true	probably false	definitely false
A woman minister who is married can fulfill her responsibilities as wife and mother just as well as if she were not working full-time.	18*	35	32	15
Women ministers are likely to have higher levels of absenteeism from work than men.	5	25	42	28
Women ministers are likely to change pastorates more often then are men.	3	18	52	27
Being divorced would impair the ministry of a woman more than of a man.	23	29	31	17
Women who try to be both full-time ministers and also wives and mothers are likely to have emotional problems due to all the demands placed on them.	15	43	31	11
The children of women who are full-time ministers are likely to have personal problems due to lack of care and attention.	7	26	43	24
Most churches today need the strong leadership that a man is better able to give.	16	25	32	28
A woman's temperament is just as suited for the pastoral ministry as is a man's.	22	21	30	27

Table 7.2 (continued)

GENDER PREFERENCES:

	prefer a man	no difference	prefer a woman
senior minister/sole pastor	54	45	0
assistant pastor	21	75	4
performing a baptism	31	68	0
administering the Lord's Supper	28	72	0
preaching a sermon	31	68	1
conducting a funeral	36	64	1
advising you about a personal problem	26	67	7
guiding the church in a building programme	47	52	1
coordinating church staff as senior minister	42	52	7

WILLINGNESS TO STEREOTYPE:

If in fact tensions were to arise in the congregation because a woman had been recommended, which of the following actions do you think the Deacons should take?

34 stick with their recommendation and try to convince the church to call the woman
55 do nothing, but let the majority of the church decide what to do
11 withdraw the woman's name and recommend a man instead

* percent responding

their likes and dislikes for women in clergy roles, and their willingness to discriminate against women ministers within their own congregations. They include all of the measures of such attitudes that were used in all three surveys. The distributions of responses to these items show that indeed we have measured variables; the church members differed widely in the extent to which they harbor stereotypical assumptions about clergywomen, prefer men in clergy roles, and are prepared to discriminate against female candidates for clergy positions.

Bivariate Analysis

Having demonstrated that lay church members in both societies differ in several facets of receptivity to women in ministry, we return now to the question of whether societal differences account for those variations. If the similarities between the United States and England are determinative, then we should observe no significant differences between the attitudes of English and American church members. If, on the other hand, the relative innovativeness of the American religious scene makes any difference in church members' attitudes towards this kind of social change, then we should observe greater resistance to women in ministry among the British than the Americans. The correlations between measures of sexism, society, and denomination are shown in Table 7.3.

The results of correlating measures of each dimension of sexism with the US/UK breakdown are clear. There was no significant correlation between society and any aspect of resistance to women in ministry. A cross-tabulation of society with willingness to discriminate against women candidates was statistically significant by chi-square, but that association was curvilinear. The American church

Table 7.3

RANK-ORDER CORRELATIONS BETWEEN RELIGIOUS SEXISM INDICATORS, SOCIETY, AND DENOMINATION

	society	denomination	society controlling for denomination:	
			Baptists	Presb./URC
reliability stereo score	ns*	.27	.19	ns
role conflict stereo score	ns	.21	ns	.14
sacramental pref. score	ns	.09	-.14	.24
organizational pref. score	ns	.17	ns	ns
willingness to discriminate	ns**	.24	ns**	ns**

* statistically non-significant correlation

** a curvilinear relationship

members manifested both extremes more than did the English. More Americans than English said the search committee should either stick to their guns or replace the woman with a man. The British were more inclined to take the middle road -- go with a vote of the congregation. Nevertheless, the most general pattern in these results was one of no correlation. Societal breakdowns of measures of religious sexism in these two denominations were not fruitful. Variations in resistance to women in ministry were not explained in terms of societal differences.

Table 7.3 also contains correlations between measures of sexism and denomination. In this case the results tend to confirm denominational contrasts discussed in an earlier stage of this analysis, i.e. that the Baptist members demonstrated higher levels of resistance to women in ministry than did the Presbyterian/URC members. In this instance we see that the pattern holds as well when using data from both the United States and the United Kingdom.

Multivariate Analysis

Since denominational differences appeared to be consistent, we next controlled for the influence of denomination in the associations between the measures of receptivity and society to see if there was any statistical interference.

Those partials are also shown in Table 7.3. The results indicate that indeed there were interaction effects between society and denomination. The results among the Baptists alone were even more inconclusive than in the initial breakdown. There was no correlation between society and three dimensions of resistance to clergywomen. On reliability stereotyping, however, the American members were the more resistant. But on gender preferences for sacramental roles, the British emerged as the relatively sexist ones. And the association between society and willingness to discriminate against female candidates was still curvilinear. I suspect that the conclusion of "no societal difference" is still the most plausible interpretation of these patterns.

Comparable results also appeared among Presbyterian members. Most of the correlations were statistically non-significant. However, the Americans did appear to be the more sexist in terms of role-conflict stereotyping and sacramental gender preferences. And the association between society and willingness to discriminate was curvilinear. Nevertheless, societal differences between the United States and the United Kingdom did not explain much of the variation in measures of religious sexism.

At this point, it is safe to draw some tentative conclusions:

1. There is no clear relationship between resistance to women in ministry and the US/UK dichotomy. While in a few instances a correlation emerged, there was no clear pattern in terms of the dimension of sexism involved in the association. The most general pattern is one of no difference.

2. Where societal differences in resistance to women in ministry were found, more often than not they were in the opposite direction from what one would predict on the basis of prior discussions of British and American peculiarities. Given the unique history of religion in America, one would expect Americans to be the more prepared to innovate, but instead we tended to find the Americans to be the more conservative in orientation.

INTERPRETATION

What accounts for these results? Why is there no relationship between the dependent and independent variables when examining all of the cases, and patterns contrary to expectations when controlling for the influence of denomination? To attempt to answer this question, we turn to consideration of other correlates of resistance to women in ministry observed in preceding chapters.

The first of these variables is traditional religious involvement. We have already shown that the more involved church members were in traditional forms of religiosity, the more they tended to resist women in ministry on all dimensions -- stereotyping, gender preferences, and willingness to discriminate. To incorporate this factor in the analysis, we constructed an index of religious involvement by combining church participation, saying grace at meals, church contributions, and religious ideology to form a composite index of traditional religiosity. The scores on the index of religiosity indeed turned out to be related to society. Contrary to some stereotypes portraying the British as a very religious people, American church members were more involved in traditional forms of religious expression than the English (gamma=-.51).

A second possible explanation resides in status differences. In England, for example, higher status church members tended to be more sexist than low status persons. The situation was somewhat more equivocal in the United States, where income and occupation work in this way, but education tends to have a liberating effect. Overall there were status differences between the two societies. The American churches had a higher proportion of high status persons in them (according to variations in occupation, education and income) than did the British congregations (gamma=-.51).

A third factor is sex. Where sex differences exist in sex-role attitudes, it is usually the males who are the more sexist. In this study, there were proportionately more males involved in the American Presbyterian congregations than in the English groups (gamma=.15).

A fourth possible intervening variable is age. We have already shown that older persons tend to be the more resistant to women in ministry. Analysis of these data show that there were also societal differences in age distribution. British congregations had greater proportions of older persons in them than did the American churches, although the differences were not great (gamma=.13).

The fifth possible explanatory variable is contact. Where church members have had contact with women, especially in the role of their minister, they have tended to be the more receptive of women as clergy (see Lehman, 1985; and Royle, 1984). In this study, such contact with women in ministry was more prevalent among British church members than among the Americans (gamma=-.72).

The final possible control is the influence of the member's minister. Earlier work (Lehman, 1979; 1985) has indicated that members' perceptions of the pastor's attitude towards clergywomen has a strong influence on their own orientations. Among English URC members, all respondents perceived their pastor as favoring women in ministry, while far fewer of the American Presbyterians saw their minister in that way (gamma=-1.00). The opposite was the case among the Baptists, where more Americans than English tended to perceive favorable attitudes of their ministers (gamma=.24).

On most of these other correlates, the British church members were more characterized by the attribute associated with receptivity, while the Americans were associated with the more sexist-related characteristic. Thus it may prove helpful to introduce these variables into the analysis and observe their possible effects on associations between sexism and society.

An Index of Religious Sexism

To facilitate the remainder of the analysis, we combined the indicators of resistance to clergywomen into a composite index of religious sexism. Each respondent was given one point for each dimension of stereotyping and gender preference on which he/she had a resistance score greater than the median score on that index. On the dimension of willingness to discriminate, respondents received one more point if they said the search committee should withdraw the woman's name and recommend a man instead.

The resultant scores are shown in Table 7.4. The index produced a distribution of scores which was fairly similar to that obtained on the indices of each separate dimension -- skewed positively with most members having relatively low resistance scores. It separated the respondents satisfactorily in terms of their overall degree of religious sexism.

The scores on the sexism index were related to societal and denominational differences in the same manner as emerged from preceding analyses. There was no significant correlation between sexism scores and society. The correlation between sexism scores and denomination was .23, showing the Baptists to have higher sexism scores than the Presbyterian/URC members.

Table 7.4

DISTRIBUTION OF SCORES ON THE COMPOSITE
INDEX OF SEXISM

score	0	1	2	3	4	5
percent	28	25	16	15	13	4

Regression Analysis

The final step in the analysis involved regressing the religious sexism scores with the societal variable, denomination, and the other six correlates identified above. The results of that multiple regression analysis are contained in Table 7.5, which shows the results for all cases combined and for each denomination. We introduced the variables into the analysis in two stages, first including everything but the "contact" and the "pastor's opinion" variables, and then inserting those two factors into the equation as well.

The results of the first stage of the regression analysis were largely consistent with steps preceding it. There was a weak relationship between sexism score and society, and the denominational differences and the other variables were predictive of sexism as noted above. These variables accounted for about 8 per cent of the variance in sexism scores.

However, the results changed slightly when we controlled for denomination. Among the Baptists, society was not predictive of sexism scores. With the exception of sex differences, the other variables remained predictive. For the Presbyterians, society was related to sexism score

Table 7.5

MULTIPLE REGRESSION COEFFICIENTS (BETA) OF RELIGIOUS SEXISM SCORE
WITH SELECTED CORRELATES, AMONG BRITISH AND AMERICAN
CHURCH MEMBERS

FIRST STAGE:

	society	denomination	age	sex	rel. involve't	SES	R²
all cases	.05	.17	.17	.10	.13	.06	.08
Baptists	ns*	---	.12	ns	.21	.08	.06
Presb./URC	.08	---	.19	.14	.09	.05	.08

SECOND STAGE:

	society	denom'n	age	sex	rel. involve't	SES	pastor att.	had contact	R²
all cases	ns	ns	.11	.11	.08	ns	.30	.11	.16
Baptists	ns	---	ns	ns	.20	ns	.49	ns	.32
Presb./URC	ns	---	.14	.13	ns	ns	.23	.12	.13

* statistically non-significant coefficient

with the Americans appearing the more prejudiced, and the relationship was only slightly stronger than in the initial regression. And all of the other variables were in the equation as well. So at this point, it appears as though denominational differences were masking some slight variations in societal effects.

The outcome changed even more when we added the variables of contact and pastor's attitude to the model. In the equation including all of the cases, the amount of explained variance doubled over what it was in the first stage. Both society and denomination, as well as social class, were no longer predictive of sexism. Instead it was primarily a result of the effects of attitudes perceived in the pastors, along with having had contact with women in ministry, age, sex, and religious involvement. Of these influences, it seems clear that members' perceptions of their pastor's attitude towards women in ministry had the strongest effects on their own reactions.

Again, holding denomination constant produced further shifts in the pattern of predictors. Perhaps most noteworthy is the continued dominance of the effects of pastor's attitudes. The Beta coefficient increased dramatically among the Baptists, as did the amount of explained variance -- fully 32 per cent is accounted for by only two factors, pastor's attitude and traditional religious involvement. Sexism scores of the Presbyterians were also based mainly on pastor's attitude, coupled with contact, age, and sex. The amount of explained variance was also much less for the Presbyterians than the Baptists.

The dramatic effects of perceptions of the minister's attitude towards clergywomen, characterizing the Baptists more than the Presbyterian/URC members, appear to be somewhat paradoxical. On the one hand, the Baptists typically take pride in their congregational polity and make a great deal about their local autonomy and independence of thought. However, it may be that such independence is more characteristic of differences between local congregations than within them. The local minister's influence appears to be much greater among Baptists than the Presbyterians. Halsey (1986) suggests that this pattern represents a greater tendency for Baptists to be "deferential" than is found among the Presbyterian/URC members.

SUMMARY

I began this chapter with the question of whether differences in church members' resistance to women in ministry could be explained in terms of whether they lived in British or American society. We asked whether the social and cultural similarities or differences between the two societies would prevail in influencing lay church members' responses to this innovation in church leadership. The analysis of survey data from each society has given us an answer, although it is not exactly the kind of answer we anticipated. As is often the case, the situation is more complex than we expected initially.

At first glance, it appears as though the social and cultural similarities have prevailed. If there are any residual differences in readiness to innovate between the two countries, they certainly do not seem to result in any systematic differences in the prevalence of religious sexism. The results of the initial analysis indicated that there were few (if any) systematic societal differences in resistance to clergywomen among members of these two denominations. The outcome for each denomination considered alone was more inconclusive, but the basic pattern still suggested little evidence of consistent differences in religious sexism between the United Kingdom and the United States.

Controlling for the effects of other known correlates of church members' resistance to clergywomen, in the final analysis, suggested that comparative patterns of religious sexism in the two societies are due to both similarities and differences in cultural and social patterns, but not in the simplistic sense with which we began this discussion. As for similarities, variations in sexism were due to the impact of the same variables operating in religious systems in both societies. Age, sex, social class, religious involvement, actual contact with clergywomen, and the effects of one's pastor all affect receptivity to women in ministry in both the United States and the United Kingdom.

However, the differences one may observe in church members' resistance to women clergy in the two societies seem to be due to the differential distribution of these correlates in the two countries. Any possible societal differences in religious sexism which appeared in each denomination at first glance proved to be spurious. Instead those variations were due to the differential effects of those other variables operating in both societies. The two systems are basically alike in terms of what factors make a difference in religious sexism (and perhaps other forms of sexism as well), but they differ considerably in terms of the relative prevalence of those factors. Why that situation exists must await additional historical analysis which cannot be pursued here.

CHAPTER 8
CONCLUSIONS

In this volume we have examined ways in which lay church members in England are responding to the entry of women into the ranks of the ordained clergy, a movement which challenges some traditional assumptions about church leadership. As an extension of general secularizing forces occurring in other social institutions, the pressures for approving the ordination of women began at roughly the turn of the century, but they did not really gain much momentum until the 1960's and 70's. By the mid-1980's, the forces for change had succeeded in several religious bodies, where the ordination of women had been approved officially. These denominations (in this study) included the Baptist Union, the Methodist Church, and the United Reformed Church. In other groups progress was apparent, but organized resistance was still impeding acceptance of women in Holy Orders, as in the case of the Church of England.

Variations in Lay Resistance

Data from a national survey of lay church members showed a general tendency for laypersons to accept women in ministry. On each dimension more members responded positively to women clergy than reacted negatively. Only a minority viewed clergywomen in highly stereotypical terms, preferred men in most clergy roles, or said they would not accept a qualified woman as their minister. As a whole the laity appeared rather accepting of the idea of the ordination of women.

Within this overall tendency, however, there were also wide variations in the prevalence of religious

sexism.   The people in the pews differed in their
receptivity to clergywomen in at least three ways. First,
they manifested divergent tendencies to perceive women
clergy in stereotyped terms regarding women's general
reliability as church leaders and their ability to deal
with role conflicts between job and family.   Second, lay
members   differed   from   each   other   concerning   their
preferences for men in both sacramental and organizational
clergy roles.   Third, they differed in their willingness
to accept a qualifed woman as their minister, and they
demonstrated clearly varying degrees of willingness to
discriminate openly against female candidates for clergy
positions in their local church or parish.

Explaining Differences in Sexism

These   attitudinal   differences   were   not   entirely
random or idiosyncratic variations in individual members'
responses to the women-in-ministry issue. Comparisons of
the variations in religious sexism with other factors,
some of which had been found in previous research to be
predictive of divergent attitudes, indicated that the
differences in receptivity to clergywomen could be
explained in terms of several familiar frames of
reference.

1. internalization of modern consciousness:

Some of the differences in sexism seemed to be
attributable to the advent of modern consciousness.
As members adopt a broad, secular and relativistic
world view, the perspective also affects the way they
relate to traditional religious ideas and practices.
This includes their assumptions about relationships

between sex roles and religious leadership. Evidence supporting this perspective appeared in the timing of episodes of the women-in-ministry movement, the demographic correlates of the attitudes, and the associations between the measures of sexism and traditional religious involvement.

2. localistic world view:

Somewhat related to the idea of modern consciousness is the local/cosmopolitan dichotomy, especially as it refers to variations in persons' breadth of perspective or world outlook. Members with narrow and provincial _Weltanschauungen_ were more sexist than those with broad and cosmopolitan world views. This pattern applied to both their general perspective on issues and events and their concept specifically of the role of the church in the world.

3. denominational traditions:

Denominational affiliation was consistently predictive of differences in religious sexism. The members of Anglican and Baptist congregations showed more indications of resistance to women in ministry than did those in Methodist and United Reformed churches. These denominational patterns did not seem to be reducible to matters of church polity, variations in church and sect, social class composition, or predominant theological ethos, however. The only factor that may account for the denominational variations was the date on which they officially endorsed the ordination of women. The longer ago a denomination recognized clergywomen, the

more their members were receptive to women in
ministry; but the relationship was not sufficiently
clear or strong as to allow one to place much
confidence even in this pattern.

4. congregations as organizations:

Variations at the congregational level of analysis
also helped account for differences in resistance to
clergywomen. Congregations which were relatively
large, which were growing in membership, and whose
budgets were growing faster than inflation tended to
be more resistant to women in ministry than those
with the opposite characteristics. The reason for
this pattern seems to be that affluent churches do
not have to consider any departures from traditional
patterns of church leadership. They can have what
they want without much difficulty. Struggling and
marginal congregations, on the other hand, often do
have to consider the concept of women (and other
minorities) as ordained clergy if they want to have
competent trained church leadership.

5. perceptions of threats to the congregation:

Somewhat related to the congregational factors above,
some members addressed the clergywoman question from
the perspective of their desire to protect the
viability of their local congregation. This concern
affected their receptivity to women in ministry,
because the issue of women's ordination has been
cloaked in such controversy. Members who perceived
women clergy as a possible threat to congregational
solidarity and who had internalized norms to protect

the congregation from such disruptions tended to be more resistant to women in ministry than those who did not relate to their congregations in that way. The issue was salient to the former group as it appeared to affect the life of their local koinonia.

In all of these ways, it was clear that observed variations in attitude towards women in ministry did not occur in a vaccuum. Differences in religious sexism "make sense" when viewed in social and cultural context. Like attitudes towards other objects, they can be explained in terms of characteristics of the members' life space--demographic characteristics as they indicate involvement in specific sub-cultures and world views, religious commitments and denominational identification, the kind of congregation they participate in, and the ways in which they relate to their local church.

COMPOSITE PORTRAITS

Having identified these sets of characteristics associated with differences in receptivity to women in ministry, it may be useful to construct "composite types" of persons who could be expected either to accept or to oppose women as ordained clergy. Such a typology would emerge roughly as follows. The church members who tend to oppose women in ministry are likely to be older Anglicans or Baptists in relatively low status families. They could be either male or female. They are more involved in traditional forms of religious expression than most of their neighbors, i.e. they pray at meals, give money generously and prefer that their church engage in traditional evangelism instead of social reforms. They are members of large congregations which have been growing in recent years and whose budgets have been expanding nicely. Members opposed to clergywomen think the issue will generate controversy in their local church and that some members will stay away and reduce their financial contributions as a result. Such possibilities make them concerned about the future of their congregation. They also view life in local terms. They are highly involved in local affairs, and it is these local issues and events which give their life meaning. They define the "church" in terms of their local congregation. Among Anglicans, persons opposed to women in ministry take that position partly because of their desire to see reunification with the Roman Catholic Church, something which the ordination of women might impede.

By contrast, members inclined to accept women as ordained clergy are most likely to be younger Methodists or United Reformed members from relatively high status families. They tend not to be highly involved in traditional forms of religious life. They don't pray at home very much. They don't place much importance on traditional evangelism. Instead, they think the churches should be involved social reform efforts. Their congregations tend to be small struggling bodies whose numbers have been declining recently and whose coffers are getting slimmer. Although they acknowledge that the clergywoman issue is a controversial one, they tend not to be overly concerned about it. They do not think many other members of the congregation would stay away from church or withhold their contributions over it. Even if some members were to leave the congregation in relation to such matters, they would not be particularly concerned over their departure. Their concerns are centered elsewhere. They have a more cosmopolitan orientation. Rather than wanting to be highly involved in their local

community, their significant social arenas are the broader
society and the world. They tend to view their church in
similarly broad terms, i.e. not just the local church but
also the broader Christian community. Among the Anglicans
in favor of women's ordination, there are few who place
much stock in possible reunification with Rome.

It is important to remember that these composite
types are statistical artifacts. That is, they were
constructed on the basis of a series of relationships
between measures of resistance to women in ministry and
other factors considered earlier in the analysis. As such
it is important not to reify them. Often such composite
portraits mask distinctions that would be found in other
analytical breakdowns, and they can be abused by applying
them in oversimplified terms. For example, just because
two sets of variables were found associated with sexism,
it does not also follow that those predictors are
themselves interrelated. They may each be related to
sexism for highly disparate reasons. To view them
monolithically would be a misinterpretation of the
analysis and a distortion of reality.

FACTOR ANALYSIS OF CORRELATES

One way of checking out the issue of possible
interrelationships between correlates of religious sexism
is to subject them to a factor analysis. Such a procedure
can provide an empirical basis for determining which
correlates should be viewed together. It can also amount
to a way of verifying the assertion that the various
arguments and levels of analysis considered in previous
chapters do indeed deal with orthogonal sets of conditions
under which religious sexism among church members may
vary. We performed such a factor analysis, using the

principle components method of extraction, varimax rotation, and listwise deletion of missing data.

Before doing the factor analysis, however, we combined two sets of variables not summarized in the previous analysis. These were the congregational characteristics and the measures of contact with women clergy. The congregational characteristics associated with resistance to women in ministry all involved the matter of local church affluence -- congregation size, rate of membership growth, and rate of budget increase. Since it is the matter of adequate resources which underlay the three variables, we combined them into a composite indicator of "congregational affluence," with the notion of affluence referring not just to finances but also to members. Each respondent received one point on the index if he/she was in a church which was "large" (above the median size), "growing" in numbers in comparison to the community, and with a "budget increasing" at least to keep pace with inflation. The resultant scores on the index were distributed as follows:

	"struggling"			"affluent"
score	0	1	2	3
percent	13	41	27	19

The "contact" measures consisted of two items each dealing with a different way in which members could come into contact with women clergy. The first asked simply whether they had "ever known a woman minister," an item getting at some level of direct person-to-person interaction. About 61 per cent answered "yes." The second question asked whether their church had ever "considered calling a woman as pastor" in recent years, a type of indirect "contact" with clergywomen. In this case, 28 per cent replied affirmatively. The scores on this two-item index of contact were as follows:

        no contact.............41%
        one type of contact.....43%
        both types contact......16%

We then performed a factor analysis on the total set of significant correlates derived from the analysis described in preceding chapters. The list of those variables, together with the results of the factor analysis, are shown in Table 8.1.

The factor analysis of significant correlates of sexism resulted in four factors. The first factor included five items which appear to embody in common the concept of "issue salience." The questions of perceiving a threat to the congregation indicate that the impact of women in ministry makes a difference to the respondent. The reporting of a pastor's opinion says that the member has perceived the minister's announcement of an attitudinal norm (Newcomb, *et al*, xxxx) on the issue. If they have personally contacted clergywomen in one way or the other, the matter has become relevant to them. Thus it is this matter of the women-in-ministry issue becoming personally salient to the members which ties these items together in the first factor.

The second factor contained three variables -- age, social class, and congregational affluence. We shall define this factor in terms of the "affluence" aspect-- high-status individuals and high-affluence congregations apparently go together. This label is appropriate even in view of the negative loading of "age" on the factor. The negative relationship of age with the measure of social

Table 8.1

FACTOR ANALYSIS OF SIGNIFICANT CORRELATES OF RELIGIOUS SEXISM

	ISSUE SALIENCE I	AFFLUENCE II	RELIGIOUS IDENTIFICATION III	BREADTH OF PERSPECTIVE IV
stay away from church	.87	-.04	.03	.07
withhold contributions	.81	.10	.00	.15
create tension	.76	-.14	-.15	-.02
pastor's opinion	.57	-.16	-.46	-.12
contact with clergywomen	.55	-.18	.20	-.19
social class	.00	.74	-.13	-.04
age	.10	-.59	-.06	.25
congregational affluence	-.19	.49	.26	.17
internalize congr'l norms	.01	-.32	.73	-.05
religious involvement	.04	.31	.70	-.10
eccl. localism	.02	.07	-.09	.83
cultural localism	-.01	-.43	.02	.68
percent variance	22	14	12	9

class makes sense. The sample contained a large number of retired persons. These individuals would not have had the educational opportunities the younger members enjoyed, their incomes would be considerably below those of members still working, and their occupational classifications would have reflected the low-technology picture of a previous generation. As for the joint positive loading of individual social status and affluence of congregation, it is probably an artifact of the mobility of now-affluent individuals out of marginal communities which would then also have marginal parishes within them.

The third factor contained but two variables, i.e. internalization of norms of congregational maintenance and traditional religious involvement. These two indicators are labelled "religious identification." Members highly involved and those concerned about the welfare of their local church would usually have that trait in common. And these factors tend to have similar effects on religious sexism.

The fourth and final factor contains the two indexes of localism -- breadth of perspective and scope of the concept of church. This common loading contains no surprises, and it reinforces the perception of similar effects of these variables on resistance to women in ministry.

The ways in which the denominational labels loaded with other variables is instructive. We introduced each of the four denominations into the factor analysis as dummy variables. We had to insert them one at a time, because having all of them in the matrix of correlations at once exceeded the limits of the logic of the algorithms involved. Even though there were minor shifts in the loadings as each one was introduced, the above patterns were fairly stable.

The individual denominations tended to load with specific other variables as follows:

<pre>
Denomination   Loaded with:
Anglican   (-.86).........contact   (.78)
United Reformed (.79)....contact   (.73)
Baptist   (.75)...........rel. involvement (.72)
Methodist   (.79).........NONE -- loaded alone
</pre>

The loading of both the Anglican and the United Reformed classifications with the variable "contact" fits in well with previous observations.   The United Reformed Church (then Congregational) was the first of the four bodies in the study to endorse the ordination of women.   The Anglicans, by contrast, had not taken that step as of 1986.   With their loading with opposite signs on the variable "contact," it reinforces the potential importance of that variable to bring the issue to the fore.   The URC members had the most opportunity for contact, while the Anglicans had the least.   And we have already seen that the more members deal openly with the issue of women in ministry, the more likely they are to approve the idea.

The label, "Baptist," on the other hand, loaded with the variable "religious involvement."   Evidently the total range of differences in religious participation -- saying grace, ritual involvements, contributions, and ideology-- is more associated with Baptist affiliation than with the others.   Since the loadings are both positive, it also suggests that being Baptist is more characteristic of these involvements than is belonging to one of the other denominations.

It is interesting to note that the "Methodist" label did not load with any other variable in the factor analysis.   Evidently Methodist affiliation is not particularly associated with the distinctions represented by any of the factors -- issue salience, affluence, religious identification, or breadth of perspective.

Again, the general significance of the factor analysis is that it reinforces the cautionary note sounded in relation to the composite portraits of "receptive" and "resistant" members outlined above. Just because sets of variables correlate with measures of religious sexism, it does not necessarily follow that those items predict differences in resistance to clergywomen for the same reason. Subsets of variables do tend to cluster together, but most of them are relatively orthogonal to each other. Differences in receptivity/resistance to women in ministry can be explained at several levels of analysis, and none of them are reducible to the other.

MULTIPLE REGRESSION ANALYSIS

The final question to be pursued concerns the relative predictability of each correlate of sexism while controlling for the effects of the other items. As we have introduced each variable into the analysis up to this point, we have usually ignored the possible effects of others and examined each as though it were the only thing making any difference in resistance to clergywomen. The problem, of course, is that the "real world" does not operate that way. At any point in time, a set of attitudes is influenced simultaneously by dozens of forces, some of which reinforce one another while others tend to cancel each other out. Some variables will have a great deal of influence on attitudinal differences, while others will have effects which are barely detectable.

So the question becomes which variables still appear to have determinative effects on sexist attitudes when

controlling for the impact of all other factors. We
approached this issue through the use of multiple
regression analysis. We regressed a composite measure of
resistance to clergywomen with all of the variables
incorporated in the factor analysis described above, i.e.
all of the significant correlates from previous stages of
the analysis.

A Composite Index of Religious Sexism

We combined the measures of the five dimensions of
sexism which apply to all four denominations to form a
composite index of religious sexism. This step
facilitates a regression analysis. It is appropriate also
because these measures tended to relate to the various
correlates in similar ways. The index was constructed in
much the same manner as was done in the analysis reported
in the preceding chapter. Each member received one point
for having a score above the median on each of the
stereotyping and gender-preference indexes, and one
additional point for having indicated unwillingness to
accept a qualified woman as local minister. This
procedure resulted in a range of sexism scores from "zero"
for manifesting high sexism on none of these measures to
"five" for showing the sexist response on all of them.

The distribution of sexism scores was as follows:

	low sexism				high sexism	
score	0	1	2	3	4	5
per cent	28	20	17	15	12	9

This distribution indicates that we have sufficient
numbers of cases across the full range of scores to have a
measure of broad differences in sexism. The skewness of

the distribution resembles the type of skew found on the four indexes involved in the overall index. So the index of overall sexism probably represents the global picture with sufficient precision and validity to be useful in the analysis below.

Regression Analysis:

The results of regressing overall sexism score with the significant correlates derived from earlier stages of the analysis are contained in Table 8.2. As was done in the preceding chapter, we introduced the predictor variables into the equation in two steps, first including all but the "pastor's attitude" item, and then adding that one as well. We also ran regressions for all of the cases and for each denomination separately.

The first regressions expalined an average of about 20% of the variance in religious sexism scores. When all of the denominations were included, all of the variables but two (financial contributions and ecclesiological localism) were significant predictors of sexism score. The strongest relationships involved the organizational viability items and cultural localism.

As one might expect, the regressions for each separate denomination resulted in fewer significant betas. Only three variables remained in the Anglicans' equation-- especially perceptions of congregational tension, and then internalizing congregational norms and age. There were also only three variables in the Baptist group-- perceiving tension was the strongest, followed by internalizing congregational norms and religious involvement. Five variables remained as significant predictors among the Methodists, i.e., cultural localism, ecclesiological localism, age, social class, and

Table 8.2

MULTIPLE REGRESSION (BETAS) OF RELIGIOUS SEXISM SCORES WITH SIGNIFICANT CORRELATES

	age	SES	rel. inv.	cong. affl.	con-tact	create tension	stay away	reduce contrib.	intern. norms	cult'l loc'm	eccl. loc'm	pastor opin.	R^2
FIRST STAGE:													
all cases	.10	-.08	.09	.08	-.09	-.29	-.15	ns*	-.15	.20	ns	---	.20
Anglican	.19	ns	ns	ns	ns	-.30	ns	ns	-.13	ns	ns	---	.14
Baptist	ns*	ns	.16	ns	ns	-.35	ns	ns	-.22	ns	ns	---	.23
Methodist	.19	-.16	ns	.15	ns	ns	ns	ns	ns	.25	.15	---	.16
Reformed	.28	ns	ns	ns	ns	ns	-.28	ns	ns	ns	.13	---	.17
SECOND STAGE:													
all cases	ns	ns	ns	.11	ns	-.17	ns	ns	-.12	.24	ns	.49	.35
Anglican	ns	-.29	ns	ns	ns	-.35	ns	ns	ns	ns	ns	ns	.24
Baptist	-.39	ns	ns	.28	ns	ns	ns	ns	ns	.36	ns	.36	.68
Methodist	ns	ns	.21	ns	ns	.33	-.30	ns	ns	.30	ns	.53	.55
Reformed**	.28	ns	ns	ns	ns	ns	-.28	ns	ns	ns	.13	**	.17

*statistically non-siginficant coefficient
**The variable "pastor's opinion" could not be used in the URC equation, because it was a constant; i.e.; all of the URC members who had heard their pastor speak to the issue indicated his/her approval of clergywomen.

congregational affluence. Significant predictors for the United Reformed members were age, concern about loss of numbers, and ecclesiological localism.

When the "pastor's influence" variable was introduced in the second stage, several changes were apparent. First, the amount of explained variance in sexism nearly doubled. It increased by about three times among the Baptists and Methodists. Second, the effects of pastor's opinion tended to be stronger than those of any other factor. Third, several variables fell out of the equation when the pastor item was introduced. When all of the cases were included, all but five dropped out. The five remaining were the pastor item, cultural localism, perceiving tension, internalizing congregational norms, and congregational affluence. For each denomination separately, the number of variables in the equations remained nearly the same, but in some instances the identity of those factors changed dramatically. Among the Methodists, for example, with the introduction of the pastoral influence item, all of the significant predictors but one were replaced by other variables. The variables most susceptible to having their influence overridden by the influence of pastor's opinion were age and the internalization of congregational norms.

Overall, some variables representing all of the perspectives we considered in previous chapters remained as significant predictors in the regression equations. Those which had especially strong influence on sexism appeared to be the pastor's influence and the members' concern for the viability of their congregation. Factors associated with modern consciousness were predictive in 7 equations out of ten. The localism items also remained significant variables in 7 out of ten instances. The effects of religious involvement remained in only three equations. Contact made a difference in only one, and concern about loss of financial contributions did not appear at all.

SUMMARY

Most church members of these four denominations in England share basically positive attitudes towards women in ministry. They perceive clergywomen in open and flexible terms, they are satisfied to have women playing most clergy roles, and they will accept a qualified woman as their local pastor. Stereotyping, preferring males as clergy, and outright rejection of women as ministers occurs to a significant degree in but about one-third of the members.

These variations in attitudes towards clergywomen are not random or idiosyncratic. They are explainable from the frame of reference of several theories familiar to sociologists and social psychologists. The attitudinal differences were partly due to the effects of other variables operating at several levels of analysis-- adoption of modern modes of consciousness, degree of traditional religious involvement, viewing the world in local or cosmopolitan terms, denominational traditions, different types of congregations, and motivation to protect the local congregation from deleterious effects of conflict and tension.

The results of this analysis enable us to develop an image of the members who tend to respond favorably to women in ministry in contrast to those who do not. These sets of predictors should not be viewed in simplistic or monolithic terms, however, for many of them are orthogonal to each other and derive from different levels of analysis. They reflect the complexity typically associated with differences in human orientations and actions, and they are not reducible to each other.

The results of subjecting the total set of significant correlates of religious sexism to multiple regression analysis indicated that some of them have stronger and more consistent influence than others. The variable that appears to make the most difference in church members' attitudes towards women in ministry is the attitude they perceive in their own minister. This factor seems virtually to override the possible influence of other things. Also consistent in predictability are the variations in members' concerns over church viability in the face of the clergywoman issue. Member characteristics associated with the development of modern consciousness are fairly consistent predictors, as is the effect of differences in <u>Weltanschauung</u> associated with the local/cosmopolitan dichotomy.

In comparison to the strength and consistency of those factors, some others appear to pale into the background. These include contact with women in ministry, variations in religious involvement, and age.

<u>So What?</u>

Persons both pro and con the women-in-ministry debate will find patterns in this analysis both to cheer and complain about. Such responses are hardly surprising, for we have long known that partisanship influences perception of controversial issues. People tend to perceive selectively those details which tend to confirm their preexisting orientations. Nevertheless, if the work reported here has any potential for making a contribution to the discussion of women in ministry in England, then it probably resides precisely at that point.

It is my hope that the study will provide a "reality check" on possible misperceptions and overgeneralizations concerning how lay church members think and feel about the concept of women in ministry. We have as good a sample of church members as one is likely to obtain. Accordingly, the picture we have presented is probably the best indication available of how lay persons in England are dealing with the clergywomen issue. With this information in hand, perhaps denominational decision makers can now make more informed judgements and policies than they would have been able to forge without it. From the author's perspective, if that is the outcome, then the enterprise has been worthwhile.

BIBLIOGRAPHY

Allport, Gordon W., _The Nature of Prejudice_. Garden City, New York: Doubleday and Co., 1958.

Ammerman, Nancy T., "The Civil Rights Movement and the Clergy in a Southern Community," _Sociological Analysis_, 41: 339-350, 1981.

Berger, Peter L., _The Sacred Canopy_. Garden City, New York: Doubleday and Co., 1969.

_____, _Facing Up to Modernity_. New York: Basic Books, 1977.

Berger, Peter, Brigitte Berger, and Hansfried Kellner, _The Homeless Mind_. New York: Random House, 1973.

Carroll, Jackson W., Barbara Hargrove, and Adaire Lummis, _Women of the Cloth: A New Opportunity for the Churches_. New York: Harper & Row, 1983.

Chalfant, H. Paul, Robert Beckley, and C. Eddie Palmer, _Religion in Contemporary Society_. Sherman Oaks, California: Alfred Publishing Co., 1981.

Deutscher, Irwin, _What We Say/What We Do_. Glenview, Illinois: Scott-Foresman, 1973.

Dobriner, William M., _The Suburban Community_. New York: Putnam & Son, 1958.

Dye, Thomas R., "The Local Cosmopolitan Distinction and the Study of Urban Politics," _Social Forces_, 42: 239-246, 1963.

Epstein, Cynthia Fuchs, _Woman's Place_. Berkeley: University of California Press, 1970.

Etzioni, Amitai, _Modern Organizations_. Englewood Cliffs, New Jersey: Prentice Hall, Inc., 1964.

Gouldner, Alvin W., "Cosmopolitans and Locals: Toward an Analysis of Latent Social Roles," _Administrative Science Quarterly_, 2: 281-306, 444-448, 1957-58.

Haig, Charles A., "Cooperation of Men and Women," Report to the World Council of Churches by the Congregational Union of England and Wales, 1964.

Hall, Richard M., Organizations: Structure and Process. 3rd rev. ed. Englewood Cliffs, New Jersey: Prentice Hall, Inc., 1982.

Howard, Christian, The Ordination of Women to the Priesthood: Further Report, General Synod of the Church of England: C.I.O. Publishing, Church House, Dean's Yard, London SW1P 3NZ, United Kingdom, 1984.

Jacquet, Constant H., Jr., The Status of Women in Various Constituent Bodies of the National Council of Churches -- Results of an Inquiry. National Council of Churches, 475 Riverside Drive, New York, New York, 10115, 1973.

_____, Women Ministers in 1977: A Report. National Council of Churches. 475 Riverside Drive, New York, New York, 10115, 1978.

Jarman, Margaret, Women in the Ministry, Ministry Department - Sectional Meeting, Baptist Union Assembly, 1979.

Kasarda, John D. and Morris Janowitz, "Community Attachment in Mass Society," American Sociological Review, 39: 328-339, 1974.

Katz, Daniel and Robert L. Kahn, The Social Psychology of Organizations. New Delhi: Wiley Eastern Private Ltd., 1970.

Ladd, Everett C., Ideology in America. New York: Norton, 1972.

Liu, William T., "The Community Reference System, Religiosity, and Race Relations," Social Forces 39:324-328, 1960.

Lehman, Edward C., Jr., Women Clergy: Breaking Through Gender Barriers. New Brunswick, New Jersey: Transaction Books, Inc., 1985.

_____, "Patterns of Lay Resistance to Women in Ministry," Sociological Analysis, 41(4): 317-38, 1981.

_____, "Organizational Resistance to Women in Ministry," Sociological Analysis, 42(2): 101-18, 1981.

_____, Project SWIM: A Study of Women in Ministry. Valley Forge, PA.: American Baptist Churches, 1979.

MOW, Movement for the Ordination of Women Newsletter, Napier Hall, Hide Place, Vincent Street, London, United Kingdom, 1985.

Martin, David, A General Theory of Secularization. New York: Harper and Row, 1978.

McGuire, Meredith, Remarks as discussant of a paper presented at the annual meeting of the Association for the Sociology of Religion, New York City, August, 1980.

Merton, Robert K., Social Theory and Social Structure. Glencoe: Free Press, 1957.

Nason-Clark, Nancy, "Women's Experience of Ministry." Paper presented at the annual meeting of the Religious Research Association, Savannah, Georgia, 1985.

Newcomb, Theodore M., Ralph H. Turner, and Phillip E. Converse, Social Psychology: The Study of Human Interaction. New York: Holt, Rinehart and Winston, 1965.

Peterson, Larry R. and K. Peter Takayama, "Community and Commitment Among Catholics: A Test of Local/Cosmopolitan Theory," Sociological Quarterly, 25: 92-112, 1984.

_____, "Local-Cosmopolitan Theory and Religiosity Among Catholic Nuns and Brothers," Journal for the Scientific Study of Religion, 22:4: 303-315, 1983.

Petty, Richard and John T. Cacioppo, Attitudes and Persuasion: Classic and Contemporary Approaches. Dubuque, Iowa: William C. Brown, 1981.

Pin, Emile, "Social Classes and Their Religious Approaches," in Louis Schneider, ed., Religion, Culture, and Society. New York: John Wiley and Sons, 1964.

Roof, Wade Clark, Community and Commitment: Religious Plausibility in a Liberal Protestant Church. New York: Elsevier, 1978.

_____, "Traditional Religion in Contemporary Society: A Theory of Local-Cosmopolitan Plausibility," American Sociological Review, 41:2: 195-208, 1976.

_____, "Religious Orthodoxy and Minority Prejudice: Causal Relationship or Reflection of Localistic World View," American Journal of Sociology, 80: 643-664, 1974.

Rowe, Trevor T., Division of Ministries, The Methodist Church, 1 Central Buildings, Westminster, London SW1P, United Kingdom, personal correspondence, 1986.

Royle, Marjorie H., "Women Pastors: What Happens After Placement?" Review of Religious Research, 24:2 (December), 116-126, 1984.

SMWC, Society for the Ministry of Women in the Church Newsletter, 1981.

SMWC, Society for the Ministry of Women in the Church Newsletter, 1983.

SMWC, Society for the Ministry of Women in the Church Newsletter, 1985.

Seashore, Stanley E. and Yuchtman, Ephraim, "A System Resource Approach to Organizational Effectiveness," American Sociological Review, 32:6 (December), 891-903, 1967.

Shiner, Larry, "The Concept of Secularization in Empirical Research, Journal for the Scientific Study of Religion, 6:2, 207-220, 1967.

Snowman, Daniel, Britain and America: An Interpretation of Their Culture, 1974-75. New York: Harper and Row, 1977.

Sweet, William Warren, The Story of Religion in America, New York: Harper & Brothers, 1950.

Troeltsch, Ernst, The Social Teachings of the Christian Churches. New York: Harper & Row, 1931.

Yinger, J. Milton, The Scientific Study of Religion. New York: Macmillan, 1970.

INDEX

STUDIES IN RELIGION AND SOCIETY